Grieving to Believing

to

Believing

Discovering the Afterlife

Deb Sheppard

DebSheppard.com
GrievingToBelieving.com

Edited by Judith Briles, Peggie Ireland, and Dana Nieto
Cover and interior design by Rebecca Finkel, F + P Graphic Design

Library of Congress Control Number: data on file
Hard cover 978-1-7320456-0-6
Trade paper 978-1-7320456-1-3
eBook 978-1-7320456-2-0
Audiobook 978-1-7320456-3-7

Printed in USA

To Dana Nieto my soul mate in this life
and in all the future life times to come

Sophia, Jake, Chris and Thomas

In Loving Memory
Bradley W Sheppard
Mathew W Sheppard
Norma A Sheppard
Jack W Sheppard

And all those that we love in spirit

Contents

Foreword

I am often introduced to many so-called mediums, intuitives and psychics. There is nothing "so-called" about Deb Sheppard. She is the real thing.

Not only is she a very gifted talented intuitive, psychic and spiritual medium; she has an incredible amount of compassion as well, which is what this work is all about.

Deb Sheppard is one of the few mediums that I'm privileged to share the platform with and honored to call my friend. I am very, very impressed with skills, her gifts and her ability to connect with her audiences.

If you want an incredible connection with the spirit world, a healing, I highly endorse working with Deb Sheppard.

—James Van Praagh
Clairvoyant and Spiritual Medium
Author of the *New York Times* bestseller
Talking to Heaven and producer of the
Ghost Whisperer television series

Is There Light at the End of the Tunnel?

*At 48, I didn't expect to become
a widow and a single parent.*

How does a normal family regain what is *a new normal* after a tragedy?

Most families would like to go back to the way it was without a hiccup. My family couldn't. But, we found our path and created the joy once again. And, so can you.

It's common for individuals to feel guilty about having any joy and moving forward with their lives. Instead they become suspended in a warp of time … frozen in making decisions; removing themselves from things that had delivered joy and happiness; and feeling they are undeserving of life's pleasures. Stop … I promise you, without any hesitation, that loved ones who leave you behind and have crossed only desire you to be happy once again.

You may also be surprised to learn that if you want to feel your loved one, becoming happy once again will help with that process as I reveal throughout *Grieving to Believing*.

Every journey is different. My experience was mine and I cannot proclaim to know exactly what you are experiencing. For my family, this is where we were in 2008. Shocked. Grief stricken. Paralyzed. Not believing that a loved one had taken his life. You see, I am one of you.

You see, I am one of you.

Both of my children went through their grieving to believing paths very differently, and have found their own way. If their father would have stayed with us, their lives would have been very different, no doubt. His parenting and mine were at opposites, which isn't good or bad, we just had different styles. He was a strict disciplinarian; I wasn't. The children received Social Security after his death until graduation from high school, which provided financial opportunities for them.

My daughter, Sophia, graduated from high school early and entered college immediately. She put her heart, mind, and body into it while working almost full time. Within two years, she graduated and walked magna cum laude. Sophia earned her bachelor's degree in graphic design and entrepreneurship. She received many awards for her work, including one for her internship. Surprising her family, she decided to go to Calcutta, India, to help women escape sex trafficking, teaching them to heal through art.

Her two-and-a-half months in India was life changing, as well as terrifying. After her father died, Sophia revealed that he had raped her. At first, I was so shocked, I did the "normal" and wanted to deny it. I couldn't. I knew she would never say this unless it was true. My heart went out to her. The guilt I had for not protecting her was heart wrenching. How could I have allowed this to happen? No wonder Sophia wanted to escape— Calcutta wasn't far enough for what she had gone through.

As she opened up, she shared that she believed her dad thought what he was doing to her, he was doing to me. She was aware that he was struggling and that he wasn't in his right mind. Her actions began making sense—how she behaved around her father, Brad, and her choices in life. After telling me, I made sure I was available to her—we discussed it when she wanted to, but I also knew she kept very busy to keep distracted about her father. My Sophia is a very strong person. She has done so much work to heal and live a great life that she continues to create.

After she returned from India she said, "I need to do something fun." She had a plan. Sophia and her 16-year-old brother, Jake, decided to travel to Europe and do a walk-about. They were able to learn about each other, make new memories, and do more healing.

Their grandparents, Brad, and his brother Greg, all lived in Italy while their father Brad served in the Air Force. Sophia and Jake took some of his ashes and found the house they lived in to release some in this place he loved. Brad's mother Norma had passed when they had just arrived in Europe. I was able to send some of her ashes to them. My heart told me that it was the right thing to do—releasing Brad and Norma's ashes at the home they loved and had fond memories of.

Jake was able to use the travel as school credits, so when he returned he was able to continue his high school education and graduate on time.

Jake and his father were extremely close. When Brad died, he was only 11. Jake's path to and through grieving was in his personal way. As we all grieve differently, his process became his very own.

Attending school was difficult. With the unexpected death of his father, I imagine that it was too difficult to concentrate on subjects that were not important to him. It was difficult for me to carry on daily responsibilities, so I'm sure it was painful for him as a young boy. I never got upset with him. I tried to figure out how to best guide him and see his happy face once again. Even as I write this, my heart hurts for the pain he endured as a child when this should have been a wonderful time in his life.

The counselors and most of his teachers were very supportive. I even had a tutor work with Jake at school to keep him organized and focused. I needed, he needed, all the help we could get. Suddenly, I was a single parent, juggling everything that now was all on my plate. The three of us were lost. And somehow, Sophia, Jake, and I needed to heal.

School wasn't working for him. Thankfully, a good friend was a counselor at an alternative school, which had small class-rooms along with support that was adapted to each student. Jake was resistant in the beginning; he didn't want to change schools. He joined the basketball team and by his senior year became its captain. His coach really looked after him, and Jake tried hard to please his teachers and classmates. Jake rocked at the new school. It was just what he had needed.

He also had counseling. Not in private sessions, but an envi-ronment that kids could go and be with other kids who were grieving from all types of losses. For two summers, he attended Camp Comfort. It is a program for three days and two nights where attendees camp with a "buddy" ... adult volunteers who are trained to help young people grieve while still being a kid.

I loved this program and donated to it and its cause. The last day of the program, a ceremony is held where ribbons are tied around an evergreen tree by the kids. In the background, music is played and the leaders speak as well as a few of the kids. They asked Jake to share his experiences with everyone in attendance—about 150 kids, families, and the buddies. With a mic in hand, Jake was a real trooper. He spoke; he shared; he glowed. I was so proud of how he handled himself and talked from his heart. I knew his father would have been proud as well.

As we left, Jake jumped in the car and we briefly talked about his speech. He then asked if he could announce me at my events like his father had done previously. "Of course," I told him, and he did this for many years. You can even see videos of him on *YouTube* when he was 12 to 13 years old. Now, towering over six feet, he has come a long way from being that small guy with a squeaky voice.

After graduation, Jake didn't want to go to college. He wasn't sure what he wanted next. Since Europe, he had the travel bug and wanted to embrace some of the U.S.

Starting in Colorado, his next journey took him through Arizona, California, Oregon, Washington, Victoria (Canada), Idaho, Montana, Wyoming, then returning to Colorado. He lived in his car, a tent, and stayed with friends. Arriving home, he displayed beautiful long red hair and I'm sure a few more inches of height. As his mother, I loved that his energy and confidence were good. Once again, I was proud of his courage. Jake was back.

We continued celebrating holidays and in some cases kept some traditions the same as we had enjoyed as a family of four, while changing others. In the beginning, it seemed that we would put a lot of energy and thought into the marked days of Brad's birthday, Father's Day, and the anniversary of his passing. But, over the last couple of years we have honored him differently. It's not out of disrespect or that we don't love him anymore. It's just that we are different and do it differently.

We talk about him often and feel his presence throughout the year. Our lives continue to change and over time it has become more of an acceptance that he's gone. All of us—Sophia, Jake and myself—have allowed our healing to flow and change as needed for where we are in life.

You may also notice that others don't reach out as in the beginning of your experience with death and healing. It's not that people don't care; this is just how life unfolds.

For me, I continued to work hard—almost too much—and still had a strong business. For four days, I fought for my life in ICU after almost dying from pneumonia after a surgery. A few years later, I was diagnosed with partial complex seizures. My body was speaking to me: it was time to change things. I was exhausted and felt that I hadn't really grieved or been able to figure out what I wanted. As Mom, I was focused on my kids; I forgot about me.

I discovered the light that was waiting for me at the end of my tunnel.

I decided to cut the mentoring programs, and a few other programs I was teaching, because I just couldn't and didn't want to try and keep up with everything anymore. Many were upset with me. Judgment flowed and I lost several friendships, something that is not uncommon when things happen and lives change.

I don't feel my personal judgment was as centered as it should have been and felt I was struggling with many aspects in life. Some wanted to help me, but I rejected them. I didn't feel I was ready to accept help. For me, I just wanted to be left alone and shut down for a while. As I look back, I know many were hurt by my "I want to be alone" attitude. For those close to me, what they saw then was me trying to manage my healing, and I needed to.

At 48, I didn't expect to become a widow. And, I didn't expect to become a single parent, but with my belief about the afterlife and understanding that Brad was very ill, I was able to put one foot in front of the other. Sometimes stumbling; sometimes feeling I was going in circles. But I knew that I wanted to teach my children about death and how to still live. I wanted them to have the very best life they could under all types of circumstances.

And for what you are going through, I know that there is light at the end of your tunnel as well. *Grieving to Believing* will show you how to have the very best life you can under any type of circumstance.

Are you ready?

2

My Story
"Begins

After having a few glasses of wine to get my courage up,
I sat Brad down and shared my new insight
and what was going on in my head.

It was 1986 and I knew it was time for a career change. My background in business was personal insurance. I had been working for three years for a computer company and it was time for a shift.

For some reason my "gut" told me to connect with a particular company. Although this didn't make smart business sense, I only applied to this one company. After receiving a call that they were interested in meeting with me, they shared very confidently that I would be a better fit at their subsidiary company, which was known as the Insurance Center—many called it the "Country Club." My first thoughts: *Okay, I'll play the corporate game and take the job. Just get me in the door.* My intention was to move over to the bigger company and move up the corporate ladder.

It was Ann Games who hired me. We had an immediate connection and she took me under her wing. She was one of the angels that life sometimes brings us; they change our path by providing a new direction.

Corporate was right. Our office was like a country club. This was just a great mix of people who had one heck of a fun time. These friends are still in my heart, even if I haven't talked to them in years. Our building looked as if it belonged in the mountains, with big windows, high ceilings and an outside cabin appearance. We did have cubicles, but since there was so much light and it was a very open space, it was a nice environment in which to work.

Smart Career Move or Was It Divine?

Being excited about my new career, I decided to start my days early. Get to work early, learn what I needed and get moving. Living in Sacramento, California, where days can be hot, very hot, parking in the shade was very desirable. I'd snag such a spot when available. Proud to be in the office early, saying hello to all my new friends, I felt good. Then a man that I hadn't met yet stopped at my desk. With a serious look but in a kind voice, he asked, "Do you drive a black truck?"

The response came across clearly—even to this day, I can hear it: "You have parked your vehicle in my space."

Then with an edge, which probably wasn't the most intelligent career move on my part, I responded, "Are you telling me we have segregated parking?"

"Are you telling me we have segregated parking?"

With a little huff, which was meant to be a laugh, I think, he said, "Yes," and walked away.

Then I gulped, muttering, "Oh sh*t." I moved quickly to Ann's office. I asked her if the underground parking was assigned. She replied in the affirmative and then asked me where I had parked. Telling her, she said, "Move your truck."

Yes, I had taken the parking space of my new boss' boss. Yikes, not a good first impression for my hoped-to-be new career. While being raised to treat everyone the same no matter where they are from or what they have, I came to my senses and moved my little black truck. Think before you speak.

Think before you speak.

Now I was asked to meet my boss' boss. Yes, this feels positive ... and I'm just going in with an open mind. He apologized for making me move my truck and then asked if I wanted to meet for drinks later. Again, without thinking, I said, "Sure." As I left his office and starting working, it occurred to me that I am starting this new career and wondered if this was a date? Seriously, I'm looking back thinking was I really that naive? Obviously, I was!

Later, I walk into his office and asked, "Is this like a date?" Yes, I used the word "like." Well, it's a sign that I'm a girl from California. That was many years ago and many lessons learned since that day.

We went out on a date. I think it was more acceptable during that time or at least that's what we told ourselves and I'm glad we did. My first "real" date with my future husband was Old Town Sacramento. It was the same night for a local high

I now understood why I was led to this company.

school's prom. We shared our first date with a crowd of teen-agers. Throughout our life together, whenever we were out and dined where kids were dressed for prom, we would smile and silently think of our first date.

This wonderful man that showed up as my new soulmate was Bradley W. Sheppard. He became my friend, lover, and husband. My life felt blessed and I was overwhelmed with my new life. I now understood why I was led to this company and sent to work at the "country club" instead of the headquarters. It made total sense to me and I couldn't have asked for more. Remember, the year was 1986. Today, "going out" with the boss would seriously be frowned upon.

Less than a year into my new job and in love, Brad was advised that the company needed to make changes. The new direction was to merge offices, which meant our location would be closed. This, of course, was very difficult. The connections and relationships were so special. Everyone had talent and could move on, but it was the collective group that made all the talent work. We felt as if this was our family of choice.

One of the things Brad and I always shared was the enjoyment of good restaurants. He spoiled me by taking me to fabulous restaurants that he would find out about and research—long before the internet and Google. It was a big deal for us. He always made me feel special and that I was the only woman that mattered. I just couldn't believe how much I was beginning to love this man.

One of our favorites was a French restaurant. During dinner, he handed me a beautiful satin green box with a note that said, "Let's fill this box." His next words made my heart dance. He said, "I'm moving to Indiana and I want you to go with me." Still today, I have the box and the note.

We were married October 25, 1987, in an old Victorian house. The ceremony was performed by the husband of a friend who I had worked with at the previous computer company. My friend Chris—another angel along my journey—stood next to me and Brad's brother, Greg, stood up for him. We were surrounded by one hundred guests as we took our vows. Our new life as a married couple began as we packed our belongings and moved east to Carmel, Indiana.

Indiana was not my dream zip code, but we both found our way. The marriage was going very well. However, setting up house-keeping while also trying to get pregnant wasn't easy. It didn't help that we also bought the money-pit house! But, with those that move for their careers, you don't let moss grow under your feet too long, because most likely there will be change.

Ohio was our next adventure and this time I fell in love with the house we found. I had landed a job that I liked and, finally, after several years, we were expecting a baby. Life seemed to be quite amazing and I appreciated where our life had taken us. One afternoon we found ourselves relaxing on our deck that overlooked our neighbor's pasture with grazing horses and cows. It was an idyllic scene. We marveled at how our grass was so green and enjoyed watching our longtime friend, Bear, a dark red Golden Retriever, as he played and hung out in our back-yard. I loved this space. Once again, I felt we were creating a life that most only dreamed about creating. I was so grateful … how could this be my life?

Let's Go West

As the afternoon progressed, evening and wine arrived. Brad had become serious and revealed that things were not going well at his job. He would never blame anyone, but he shared that his boss didn't care for him. This seemed so out of character, but again I always believed in him. He was very smart and well-liked by his peers. Then he explained that there may be an opportunity in Colorado, and would I consider it? Without hesitation, I said

YES! This would be closer to my family and his. It just felt right. I was excited about the possibility of moving once again, even though I was pregnant.

Our daughter, Sophia, was born January 8, 1993, and six months later, we were living in Colorado. Life seemed to be on track once again and we began to live the all-American dream. We felt very blessed.

I struggled with finding anyone other than Mary Poppins with a Louis Vuitton carpetbag.

After we relocated, I was looking for child care and a new job. I had waited and longed for Sophia. I struggled with finding anyone other than Mary Poppins with a Louis Vuitton carpetbag with whom I was willing to leave her. I was in emotional turmoil. After a job interview to transfer from the same company I had worked for in Ohio, I walked out knowing that I absolutely could not work in corporate America any longer. So I decided to open a childcare business in our home.

Interesting how little things are actually bigger than we think after time passes and we reflect.

We lived in an upper middle-class neighborhood where many families needed drop-off child care or teachers who worked year round and required full-time service. It was my new niche and I was once again grateful that I was able to stay home and care for families in my community. It was a win-win for my new life.

It Keeps Coming

After being in Colorado for a few years, Brad's career took another hit and we were once again going through another corporate change. There were two hurricanes that year back-to-back, one in the Carolinas and the other in Hawaii. Unfortunately, the company he worked for insured many properties in both locations so it took a significant financial hit. The company began to downsize.

We both loved Colorado and the life we were building together, moving back to the Midwest to reinvent his career wasn't an option for either of us. It wasn't long after this event that I became pregnant with our second child, born August 3, 1997. Of course, this one came as a beautiful surprise with little effort.

The journey that began was extremely difficult, but we were optimistic at the start. Brad and I both believed that we could start new by him being self-employed. Taking this as a sign to be your own boss—another American dream. He had a master's degree, was great at statistics, honest and good to others. We had received a payout from the company that provided a good cushion and we had a little money in our retirement.

Well, it wasn't meant to be. When I began to really look back on our lives after his death, I now can say I noticed a change right before we left Ohio. It wasn't recognizable then, but it's always an "aha" afterward. He put on a great front and I still believed in him and that we were going to get through this. We both believed we would. He wanted to keep the house which was and still is a big expense.

My heart sank as my stomach was showing this new life.

Things were not easy. While expecting our second child, he had taken a (temporary) job with UPS working nights stocking trucks with packages to be delivered—a far cry from when he was "the boss." It was hard work, especially at the age of 42. They provided insurance which was a must for us during this time. I was doing child care, expecting, and he was working nights. In reality, we were barely making ends meet and we barely saw each other. He was ashamed that after his successful career he was working nights packing up trucks. None of our friends knew where he was working or what he was doing. For me, I didn't care what he did as long as he was okay and we could provide for our family.

One night he came home after an evening shift, we sat on the end of our bed, and he told me he had quit his job. He said that the work felt beneath him and he couldn't do it anymore. I remember as if it were yesterday, my heart sank as my stomach was showing this new life. We weren't in any way financially capable of taking care of all our needs, but I didn't say a word.

Was I to trust his decisions as I had in the past? I was beginning to question my feelings. To this day, I'm not sure why I didn't challenge him, other than I was in shock. And he had always taken care of us.

As time passed, we had gone through all of our savings and had refinanced the house enough times that there was no cushion. We filed for bankruptcy and it seemed to be one of the most difficult times in our marriage. We didn't want to not pay our debts. How could we have gotten here? Was it the choices we were making that kept us going down this path?

While doing child care, one of the parents had listened to part of my story. Her brother owned a mortgage refinance company and thought Brad might be a good fit. Well, we felt grateful because an opportunity was opening up. These were good people and they wanted to help us, and they were open to teaching Brad the ropes. Having a degree in economics, it wasn't going to be a tough road for him to learn the business.

The Spiritual Path

I began looking at a spiritual journey. I started meditating and looking for other answers to our life. My friend, Chris, had flown out from California. When she arrived, I began sharing our situation and she mentioned Feng Shui. I was very open-minded, but had no idea what she was talking about. As females like to do, we went shopping and stopped at the book store. The book I pulled out and still have to this day is *The Western Guide to Feng Shui* by Katherine Terah Collins. Little did I know that it would take me on a new journey.

During this same time, I went to a metaphysical fair. Desperate to hear that we were going to get back on our feet once again, I was hungry for information—anything that would reveal a path for us to take. We were good, hard-working people. So why was this happening to us? My friend, LaVern, was working the fair and she had me see one of her friends, a psychic. She said that she didn't feel that the perfect job was coming for Brad. Then, she asked me a question I'll never forget: *Why wasn't I sitting on the other side of the table doing readings?*

> **I was hungry for information—anything that would reveal a path for us to take.**

I was frustrated with her response about Brad and her question that had nothing to do with why I came to see her. I thought, *that's not why I am here. What do we need to do to get back on track?*

She said nothing else, or at least that's all I chose to remember.

Feng Shui

I decided that Feng Shui was our answer. I could take control of our lives again. If you are unfamiliar with Feng Shui, it's an ancient belief about energy or Chi. It is the flow of things and how it responds to our life. Many that practice Feng Shui may not respect the Western version as equal to the ancient beliefs, but hey, I was a western girl and it was something I could do. So, it all began.

The first thing I started doing was cleaning up clutter. Brad wasn't a hoarder, but he didn't throw much out. I am known for that as well. But don't we see other people's things as "junk," yet not always our own?

After bagging up things of his, I began carrying the stuff to the trash. While walking outside, I fell down hard and scraped both of my knees. Later, I learned that you don't take other people's things without their permission; I didn't have his permission. My intention was to help him with "his career" without his blessings. Rarely does that work.

Brad was always supportive of what I liked to do or needed. But still, I didn't tell him what I was doing with "his things." I continued on my crusade. This couldn't hurt and I was feeling as if I was taking steps to get our family back on track. Feng Shui became pretty easy for me. I could feel the energy and understood how it worked. I even considered becoming a Feng Shui consultant. Especially now, with two children, the work as a childcare provider was getting harder on my body and patience.

It felt like I was in slow motion.

Then one day after lunch, when all the children were down for nap time, and I was cleaning up things, I could feel someone around me. It was not a living person and I wasn't scared. It felt like I was in slow motion. Maybe you have been in a car accident where you see what is going on, but there is nothing you can do. It happens so fast, but amazingly you can recall the details. It's what I felt like. And, I felt as if it was my friend Susie's father, who I had never met. She owned a salon and I called her and shared what I experienced, telling her messages from her father. Several hours later, I recall thinking to myself *that was weird. I need to call Susie back.*

I did call her back and she was still a little shaken. I apologized to her and her response was, "I needed to hear that. My father was a good businessman and he taught my brothers how to run a business, but not me. I would have asked for his help now since I'm learning how to be a business owner."

Little did I know that my life would dramatically change. Well, that's when the flood gates opened and her father and others began showing up.

The voices kept coming and I was overwhelmed by what I was experiencing.

I didn't know what was happening, so I went to the library and checked out dozens of books. The internet wasn't like it is today. I wouldn't always read entire books, letting myself be guided to chapters I was drawn to or believed were needed. That's when I realized I was a medium. But what did that mean and what do I do with it? Even with many losses in my life, I wasn't drawn to going to a medium or connecting with my own loved ones. So why was this happening?

Well, the voices kept coming and I was overwhelmed with what I was experiencing. After having a few glasses of wine to get my courage up, I sat Brad down and shared my new insight and what was going on in my head. I revealed that I could hear the voices of dead people and I wanted to let him know. Brad's response was funny, which he often was. "So you're not pregnant? If you are, we are way too old for another child."

I laughed and said, "No baby, but how do you feel about this revelation?"

He replied, "Deb, you have always been very intuitive and I think it's great."

WOW! Yet I couldn't help wonder how he could be so supportive of this when I was still in disbelief. But I was truly thankful for his positive words. My husband was wishing me well on a new trajectory.

3

Becoming a Medium

*Things that I was seeing and hearing
totally surprised me.
And to this day, they still do.*

I can't remember the exact day that I heard my first voice from the other side, but I was around the age of 38. I did have a few experiences that I can remember prior to that, but I never put together that people could actually talk to "Spirit". This wasn't accepted or taught in school. It certainly wasn't a subject talked about in my family or circle of friends. Growing up, I was raised as a Jehovah's Witness. My father was an elder and we went to meetings three times a week. I also was preaching door-to-door on Saturdays. Learning to take a spiritual path was at odds with my childhood rearing. However, I hadn't been practicing my faith for years. As a matter a fact, I was dis-fellowshipped when I was 23. This meant I was no longer a member of the organization. And I wasn't allowed to see family and friends who were still members.

One memory that I have was when I was a teenager. One morning before school, I walked into the kitchen where my mother was making breakfast—as she always did—and she asked how I had slept. My response was that I had dreamt of Elvis Presley dying in the bathroom. My mother had a wonderful sense of humor, a trait I inherited that has been essential in the work I do, and responded with "Would you like sugar or syrup on your French toast?" What an interesting pivot. But what did I expect her to say in response to something like this in 1972? *Bewitched* and *I Dream of Jeannie* were very popular TV shows and pure fantasy: but talking to the dead? If not unheard of, certainly not mainstream! Just a little side note: My daughter Sophia was born on Elvis's birthday January 8, 1993. Doing what I do, this synchronicity added to my understanding of what I do as a medium.

Life takes yet another turn. So, knowing that I'm a medium, what does that mean and how do I move forward? I shared this with a few friends and they wanted me to do a reading for them. A reading? I really had no idea what that looked like, but I just trusted it. Things that I was seeing and hearing totally surprised me. And to this day, they still do.

I kept what was happening and what I was doing under wraps and shared only with people I felt comfortable with. Not everyone thinks this is awesome.

Some with certain religious beliefs felt all this was just too weird. If this wasn't me doing it, I would probably think it was just too weird as well. In most cases, as I transitioned into my work as a medium, I wasn't too offended by others' curiosity, objection, or fear around my new path. I still believe today that skeptics are always welcome. Most people are smart enough to make their own decision after having a session with me.

It hasn't always been easy when you have someone reject, disagree, or not believe. But as I shared earlier, if I wasn't the one getting the messages, I could very well be in the skeptics' same space and beliefs.

The Launch

At this point, I didn't know anyone else who could give me support or answer all the questions that came into my mind while learning, receiving, and embracing my new venture. But, this too had a divine intervention that came into our life. A friend had called to tell me that the psychic John Edward was going to be in town at a local hotel and tickets were being sold. I called Brad and asked what he thought of attending the event. He supported me as usual and said, "Go for it." The tickets were expensive, especially for where we were, but we got them and went.

The hotel was packed. It seemed liked there were at least 1,000 people in attendance. John Edward did the show with another medium and the event was about two hours long. I didn't attend to have a reading, but knew I needed to attend to see a medium in action.

John Edward was in the back of the room, while the other medium was on stage. I thought to myself, *Should I go talk to him?* I decided it was a boundary and how strange it would feel for me to ask him questions. I was nervous and curious as to "why" we spent $500 to attend and I felt there was no reason as to why.

During the break, Brad went out to our car and I just paced, watching those who were in attendance and trying to figure out why I needed to be there. The room was hot, and you could feel the sadness of the people and their desire to hear from their loved ones. With many hundreds of attendees and only two hours of readings, it wasn't hard to figure out that very few people would actually hear from their loved one on this night.

After the event was over, we got into the car and drove home. I was frustrated as to why we had spent the money. We didn't have to attend. I continued to feel disappointed as to why I had gone. Then I started to look at my frustration and the "why" from different angles. My first thoughts were: Maybe it was to see how many people wanted to hear from their loved one. Maybe it was to let me know there was a need. And maybe I could help these individuals in some way. But, I had no idea how that would unfold.

> **He never changed the station to *KOSI 101.1*.**

Brad and I started to process what occurred and how I felt. As we were talking the radio was on *KOSI 101.1*, a light rock station. I didn't listen to the radio much unless I was in the car. While we were listening to *Rashke After Dark* with her guest, Sid the Psychic, I told Brad that I was going to call the station the following day. I was going to share our experience at the event and perhaps they would be open and interested.

It wasn't until years later that Brad shared with me that he had gone to the car during the break at the John Edward event and was listening to a Rockies baseball game. He never changed the station to *KOSI 101.1*. The game was on an AM station and *KOSI* was an FM station. Fate was on our side once again.

Now let's remember, I was still doing child care; had not established a practice; and was still very green as a medium, if that's what I was. I just felt pulled to this and besides—where we were now—what could it hurt? I called the station and the receptionist transferred me to Program Manager Rick Martini. It turned out that he was from the East Coast and had helped other mediums and psychics on the radio. Was this another divine moment?

He asked me to give him a reading, which I did a few days later. It must have been good enough, because he encouraged Rashke to meet with me. Her aunt was a psychic and she had been around many individuals who claimed to have some type of intuition. She had even lived at an Ashram for a period of time. So, this wasn't out of her realm.

After about a month, she came over to my home when the kids were napping and I "tried" to give her a reading. She seemed frustrated with what I was saying. It wasn't making sense to her. This is when trust is truly at the forefront. I stayed with what I was getting and just kept my fears in another room.

I had told her there was a problem on the roof of her car on the passenger side. She said it was a new car and there wasn't anything wrong with it. There were many other things I shared that she responded to with a no. I just took a deep breath and thought, if this is meant to be I need to trust it.

Well, it wasn't long after my reading that her new convertible was having trouble in the very spot I had told her about. She began to recall things that I had said, and she was able to validate. Our relationship began as new friends. Rashke was in Italy on September 11, 2001, and like all of us she was deeply affected by the tragic event. After her flight back, she reached out to me and asked if I would come on her show the following Friday. Of course, my answer was yes.

There was no doubt that I was nervous. I had never been on the radio and at this point,

Your life just changed forever. Are you ready?

I didn't have an established business. My thoughts went in two directions. Either this is going to go very well, or it's my 15 minutes of fame that I hope no one would remember. Rashke was very clear about what I needed to do and was a great teacher. She had a volunteer taking the incoming calls. There were five lines of callers and he would write down the name and tell me who was waiting for a reading. He documented that I had completed 52 readings that evening. Of course, only about 15 were actually on the air because it was a show with music and I was on in between songs.

Rashke looked at me and said, your life just changed forever. Are you ready? I didn't realize until years later what these words truly meant. She was right. And once again, I was grateful to another earth angel who was brought into my life.

As I drove home at almost midnight, I called Brad and told him I was quitting child care and this was the direction I was going. It was time for a fresh start, one that my very core was pulling me toward. Keeping my fingers crossed, I was going to trust this was a divine direction for me to take. I never looked back, and my life did change forever.

I became a regular on Rashke's show that continued until I was featured on the morning show, first with Murphy and Jo Myers, then Murphy and Denise on KOSI 101.1. I was blessed to have been a guest for 15 years. Rashke also connected me with another producer at Jones Radio and I connected with Dave Otto who I did a syndicated radio show with for more than six years—150 stations nationwide. Rashke and I were divinely connected in this lifetime and I appreciate her support to this day.

The psychic was right, I needed to be giving readings. It just took me time to understand what that all meant.

Business began to soar. It grew to creating classes; mentoring; inspirational speaking; working with detectives on homicide cases and missing people; to name a few. Many opportunities were coming into my life and I couldn't believe how my life was unfolding, and how wonderful I felt. Stability had entered our lives; the financial pressure was off.

I was happy that I could provide for my family, while doing something that I believed made a difference in the lives of others. But life began to take another turn that wasn't expected. I was very distracted with this new work. And at the same time, Brad was going through changes that would deeply affect all of us.

He was still struggling at the mortgage company. Just how much I did not find out until later. This was during the time when everyone was refinancing their homes; everyone was banking on earning larger incomes. For Brad, his lack of performance stopped him from creating the business he wanted and needed.

Since we had two children at home and my business was skyrocketing, I asked him if he would take over the administration duties and help with the kids and the house responsibilities. He was excited to get out of the mortgage business and immediately said a resounding "Yes!"

We were now business partners and our life seemed to be turning around after several years of the unknown. The psychic was right, I needed to be giving readings. It just took me time to understand what it all meant.

It was the first time in my life I felt I understood my life and felt as if I had a support system and a purpose. I could help my family and those who wanted to heal from losses. I felt truly blessed. People came into my life and gave me insights and tools that continued the momentum. It was an amazing time and I experienced so much. I am grateful for the teachers that came into my life. I sometimes feel I didn't know how to show my appreciation during those times.

After a few years, Brad's energy continued to change. He was no longer the man I fell in love with. He didn't seem like the father of my children; he distanced himself from all of us. Things began to drastically change. As I look back, it had started when our daughter was born and we moved from Ohio to Colorado. I didn't realize it then, but there were telling signs.

4

The Spiraling Deepens

My husband didn't see what he was doing
or know who he was.
I wanted my "normal" back.

Brad began to spend a lot of money on things we didn't need. His behavior and his organization skills changed, and I didn't know how to communicate with him. Everything seemed different. If I confronted him or tried to discuss what he was doing, he would become upset, thinking I was confused, perhaps I was stressed, or I was expecting too much. So I would back off.

We were working hard. We decided to take the kids on a short weekend vacation to the 5-Star Broadmoor Hotel in Colorado Springs as a celebration—a vacation that we hadn't been able to do for years. For some reason, the service was sub-par at one of the restaurants—certainly unusual for this hotel.

Brad had a "big" voice, one that could carry across any room. All of a sudden he started yelling at the manager in the middle of the restaurant. Not knowing what to do, I took the kids and headed out the door to escape the scene. Back in our room, Brad didn't "get" why I was upset. He thought he handled the issue just fine. The kids and I just tried to act as if nothing happened, so we could just enjoy this short vacation. Biting my tongue, I let it go. The behavior I was seeing on a regular basis had become the new normal and I wasn't liking it.

Our happy life had become a mere shadow

There were changes with the kids as well. Sophia had health issues and was very self-absorbed with things that at the time didn't make sense. She was a teenager, but I knew it was more than that. Brad attached himself to Jake and as a result, Jake felt his purpose was to make his father happy. He even gave up time with friends because he was worried about his dad.

We had gone from a successful partnership to being unable to financially take care of ourselves to things returning to financial security once again. I could feel trouble brewing, but I didn't want to admit that life was going to change once again.

I felt as if I was throwing my entire soul into the depths of the fire.

I became a hawk watching over Sophia and worried that Jake was giving up his childhood to protect his father. I was trying to manage the energy around my children, continue my business, and cover all of our expenses. In the meantime, I was watching Brad spiral into someone I didn't know. I felt I was living with a stranger and he didn't see that anything was wrong.

As time passed, I saw more and more things I was concerned about. Clients would show up at the wrong time or two clients at the same time. Now he was spending money that we didn't have. That's when things began to escalate.

I was blessed with dear friends—one who was a psychologist and one a therapist. They were instrumental in helping me recognize what I was dealing with. When you are in love and have a family, it's likely you don't want to believe there are issues. I sure didn't. I just wanted my life to be healthy, normal, and safe. But that wasn't my life any longer, and I had to accept this reality.

I felt as if I was throwing my entire soul into the depths of the fire. The memory of the magical life on our deck in Ohio was never to be again. Brad had lost his strength and spirit. A transition had happened and I was the strong one now who had to pull this family out of this spiraling mess.

It was early February and the kids were worried about their father. At the same time, I was trying not to let them take on the responsibility of their father's actions. They revealed that he had purchased another new computer while watching an infomercial. I could feel the anger come up and knew that this was the beginning of the end of our marriage. Since the business was becoming successful and I was working so many hours, I was missing my life with my kids. And now, my husband didn't see what he was doing or know who he was. I wanted "normal" back with my kids and my husband. But that wasn't happening. My resentment grew.

I can see it in my mind like it happened yesterday. As soon as the latest new computer arrived, I confronted him in the kitchen. My pressure cooker couldn't take it any longer. My voice was stern and to the point, and I let it out, saying, "It's time for a break. I want a divorce."

Brad was totally shocked and couldn't believe his ears. I was very clear that I couldn't do this any longer. He moved out for a month into a temporary situation. We had stayed in places like this before—when you relocate and are looking for housing, you stay in a hotel that has a small kitchen and a few things like home. I think he believed "I" needed a little time to cool off and thought I was just stressed and blamed him for it. In his mind he thought the things he was purchasing were for the family. Believe me, neither our children nor Brad and I needed nine TVs or a dozen computers.

It was the time when I began to grieve.

After about 30 days, he showed up unexpectedly at the house—too soon but eager to come back to his life again. After an exchange of a few words about his coming back, he asked me if I had been able to get into a better space, so we could move forward. Of course, I was amazed at his lack of understanding that he was the one that needed to make shifts and he was expecting me to get it. I couldn't believe it.

I was lost

This is when things became more extreme. I asked him to move to the basement. Our master bedroom was on the first floor and the kids were upstairs. It wasn't the best of situations, but I knew that I needed space from him. He wasn't happy about this and I also felt myself in a place of the unknown. With so much responsibility now and not understanding who this man had become that I fell in love with long ago, I was lost. Although not aware of it at the time, I had begun to grieve for the man that I had married, even though we were in the same house. I had always believed that we were supposed to grow old together. This wasn't the life I wanted. It felt as if I was going through the motions, but I didn't have any control.

At this point I didn't know how to reach him. I would say things and his responses didn't make sense. I felt I was on the TV show *The Twilight Zone.* My heart ached. I desperately wanted to understand my situation so I could fix it. Many times I asked him to see a doctor and get help, but he didn't believe he had a problem. He told me it was me. Again, my heart ached. I decided to write him a letter to explain what I was feeling, thinking if he read it and had time to process the words, then we could really have a meaningful talk.

Well, my intuition this time didn't pay off.

He wouldn't talk to me and it became the beginning of the end. I mentioned that maybe we should bring someone in to help us since he was making so many mistakes with booking appointments and wasn't as effective in the business anymore. The only thing he heard was that I fired him with a letter, even though I had tried on several occasions to talk to him. That's when I realized that he would never be able to function as a partner where we could both support a family. My heart sank even deeper. I understood that the situation was going to continue to get worse.

This is when I had to talk with friends and family. I was pushed to draw the line in the sand. I had two young children, a home and responsibilities, and a husband that I could no longer communicate with—a husband who was unable to understand our situation.

I struggled with the choice I was about to make, knowing it would not be received well. But in my mind, this was the only healthy choice I could make.

At this juncture, I told Brad once again I couldn't do this any longer. I was exhausted and didn't have the energy to support this marriage. He was furious. With my frankness, along with the letter, he became outraged. I was anticipating this reaction because of his previous behavior, but I was also scared for myself and the kids. I felt we were in danger. With mental illness, you truly do not know what to expect.

Being very afraid and clueless as to what he was going to do, the emotions that ran through me were difficult to contain. I knew that I could not wavier. What was next was up to him and I had to listen to my soul and trust my gut. This was an emotionally difficult challenge, one of those times in your life that your gut tells you that you have to stay strong and no matter what, you cannot let your guard down.

Brad did move to the basement and we tried to make the kids feel as if everything was normal. I will tell you that you can never hide it from your kids or pretend that this or any separation is normal. I was too busy trying to manage what was in front of me from minute to minute to understand this at the time.

I had many conversations with him about finding other work and trying to reconnect and even discuss his depression. But Brad wouldn't accept that he was depressed and didn't understand why I had once again fired him from his responsibilities of helping the business. He kept bringing the letter up.

His logic was out the window. I felt I didn't have any control to heal this craziness that was in front of me. This had been the man who helped me feel supported and loved. How could this be possible that now he did not even try to make things better for himself. I was in a losing battle with no hope or direction. At times, I felt that I could not breathe. I only knew

I had to keep pushing things, so we could have a resolution. But was I willing to take my life to a place that didn't have a happy ending?

The line in the sand was made

It was the moment of truth and it wasn't a pretty picture. I pushed for Brad to find a job that could support him and told him that I would help him financially. He didn't respond well, and I knew that would be part of this process. He told me how hard it had been and said it was obvious he couldn't do anything, this coming from a well-educated man from a stable family. He could not remember all the things he had been and done that made me fall in love with him. Those memories of his past—our past—was gone, or hidden away in the recesses of his mind.

He wasn't my Brad any longer; I had lost my beloved Brad. I wasn't sure where I was supposed to go—what I was supposed to do. That's when I realized for the first time I buried my husband, the father of my children and my soulmate. It was the time when I began to grieve.

The months ahead were only the process of Brad's passing. It's like a cancer. You can fight it, but which one wins? I sensed that if he didn't get the right help and understanding, the end result wouldn't be a good outcome. What choice did I have? Our life was upside down.

This is when I realized that the only person capable of changing this situation was me and at that time. I questioned who would understand. There was a small handful of people who had seen what was going on and continued to provide clarity. When you are living with someone with mental illness on a daily basis, you keep trying to tell your head that things will get better—as if you have the flu and in a few days, it will only be a memory. It's so unhealthy and you can't see it as clearly as those who are looking in.

Things continued to escalate. The negative energy was so thick you could cut it with a knife. I felt I was walking on egg shells and I was constantly fearful. I would lock my bedroom door at night feeling that at least I was doing something to protect myself. I considered moving out with the kids, but I realized it was for him to find his space and he needed to find work.

Those close to us could see him getting more and more angry with his situation. Brad had always been good at history and math and I suggested that he get a teaching degree. That way he would have time with the kids. His parents also suggested it and were willing to help. They invited him to stay in their home in New Mexico while getting his degree. He wouldn't have any of it.

I read *How Starbucks Changed My Life* by Michael Gates Gill. It's a story of a very well-educated, successful man who had also been let go from his company. While struggling in and out of desperation, he took a job at Starbucks. One morning, I asked Brad to read the book, hoping he'd see that we all have times in our life that we go to places that we don't expect. I even suggested that he consider a Starbucks opportunity as a restart for him that could bring us health benefits, saving our family over $1,000 a month.

Well, that again was used against me. "How could you ask me to work for Starbucks? It would be the same as working for UPS. All this is beneath me."

No job is beneath anyone; it's about doing what we need to do. His energy was becoming odder. He would walk in a room and touch the end of the table, walk around a few doorways, then walk back into the same room and touch the other side of the table. He would do this several times in a row. I just watched and worried about his logic and how much anguish he was most likely in.

He would say to me, "You help so many people. Why can't you help me?"

As painful as this was to hear I would tell him that this wasn't something I could help him with. I would repeatedly say, "You need professional help." Our internal medicine doctor was also a neighbor and friend. "Ask our doctor about your situation. You will be seeing him soon for your annual checkup." He never did; he hid it all. He wanted everyone to believe life was good. There was nothing wrong.

It was now October 2008, and it would be our twenty-first wedding anniversary. My parents lived in Northern California and from time-to-time we would fly the kids out to stay with them during school breaks or the summer. My brothers also lived there with their kids, so it was a great time with cousins— swimming, camping, and being spoiled.

Brad took them to the airport on October 23 and gave the kids a big hug, even mentioning to Sophia that she may be getting a car for her 16th birthday. Sophia thought that was odd, but then she wasn't surprised since she had heard outlandish promises over the course of the year that had never happened.

At that same time, I was hosting a two-day workshop and was totally consumed with running the event. I felt really good that the kids would be with my family and were getting away from the stress we were all living in.

Typically, after some of the events I would do, I would take out the individuals that supported the workshop as a thank you. A friend at the time, Jan had worked alongside me for years and after an event, we were in a space we often felt that I called "altered" from all the energy of the event. For some reason I was more aware of things that evening. As we sat down to order, she looked across the table at me and with a stern look, told me that I couldn't go home that night.

Jan is one person I would take seriously when she would give me advice. She is one that had seen Brad's behavior change over the years and was very concerned about all of us. She was also the one who took over Brad's responsibilities, which didn't sit well with him. She was there again to support me. I responded by saying, "I'll be fine, don't worry." Others at the table began to chime in, saying, "Why not listen to Jan?" At this point I'm thinking to myself, *this doesn't make any sense.*

I agreed to stay at Jan and Billy's house that night. Jan and Billy had been partners for about the same amount of time Brad and I had been married. Maggie was also a long-time friend and went with me to make sure things would be okay at my house.

When we walked in, Brad was in the upstairs family room watching sports on TV. He had made popcorn and was drinking Scotch. This wasn't unusual, but his energy was high, and he actually was smiling. I still remember it as clear as if it was yesterday. The house seemed lighter and noisy, but in a good way. For a few minutes I questioned my decision to leave that night but knew in my gut that I had to trust my friends. I was still too close to the situation. I told him I was having a girls' night sleep-over at Jan's. He didn't say much.

The next day, we did girl things to stay distracted—pedicures and shopping. I had called the kids and they said that their dad had called them, and everyone sounded good, especially with the year we had. As Jan was driving, I called Brad. Our last discussion was that he had found a place to live and he would be moving out soon.

He answered the phone and said he would be out by the 27th as we had discussed. It was a matter-of-fact conversation and one that made me think that perhaps things would get better when he was on his own.

When I asked him what he needed to take and what I could do to help him move things, he told me he had it under control. I had recalled a number of large black trash bags of things that I assumed he was moving to his new place, but I didn't ask him, afraid he would once again get angry and tell me that I didn't need to know. Since conversations never went well during this time, my thinking was the less said the better.

I ended up staying another night with Jan and Billy. We talked and they helped me process. They had a hot tub, so I went out into the night and sat looking up at the stars and wondering where all this was going. Wondering why he just wouldn't get help. I felt relaxed for the first time in months and knew the kids would be having fun, distracted from our chaos. I believed Brad was doing what he needed to do for him.

My alarm went off that next morning around 6 a.m. I had clients that day and wanted to get a head start. I picked up my phone and there was a text from Brad. The only thing I felt was total shock. I ran into Jan and Billy's room without knocking and asked them to read Brad's text. It said,

I'm sorry things had to happen this way, but it's for the best.
This is where you can find my body.

Of course, every emotion ran through my heart and body, knowing that he made such a painful choice and knowing the pain he certainly had suffered. My heart raced to my children as I knew that their lives would be forever changed. He killed himself just two days after our twenty-first wedding anniversary. Life instantly changed and now any hope for healing or reconciliation was gone.

Jake was 11 at the time and Sophia was 15.

Brad W. Sheppard was 54 years old, born August 11, 1954, and died October 27, 2008.

5

Telling My Children ... Telling Your Children

*If you can give yourself permission
and give it time, your heart
will speak to you with a gentle voice.*

After confirming that Brad had died, I knew I had to pick up the phone and call my parents. My friends were so helpful, taking care of so many things. And my friend Robin was making flight arrangements for my parents and children to fly back to Colorado. My parents were in shock and I asked them not to tell the kids. I would tell Sophia and Jake when they arrived back home. My concern was that while on the flight home it would be overwhelming, and I didn't want to put my parents or my children through an unnecessary ordeal.

I tried my best to keep my children protected and not put them through any more pain than what they had already endured. We parents learn that each of our children is unique. How each manages things may be completely opposite of another sibling. There is no perfect way of sharing the news that someone has died, but especially if that person died by suicide—and that someone was his or her father.

What they were told was that their dad had an accident and they needed to come home. Of course, they wanted to know what happened and to hear about the details. Sophia had a dream the night before her father's passing and knew right away what had happened. She kept it from me until after they flew home. From time to time, she and I discussed that since he was so unstable, he may do something in desperation—maybe suicide or another happening that would cause his own death.

When their plane landed, we had two cars with friends for support. Sophia had brought a girlfriend with her and her friend's parents arrived knowing what had occurred earlier that day.

Sophia was Sophia. Never quiet, her personality bubbled over with questions as we settled into the car. She persisted with them, but my parents stayed on my game plan. Jake was frustrated, trying to call his father but getting no response.

Your father has died.

The kids were fairly upbeat and hungry. We headed to a drive-thru and finally, home. I sat them down in the family room—with adult friends at their side. Taking a deep breath, I said, "Your father has died."

At that time, I didn't share how or any details. My heart told me to hold off on that information. Sadness permeated the room. As my words sunk in, they were overwhelmed with sadness and could not believe what they had just heard.

I don't remember when Sophia asked, "How"—whether it was that evening or days later. She had shared her dream with me and we talked as much as we could at the time. On the other hand, Jake didn't want to know, and I decided to honor that decision. Jake and his father were extremely close, and of course, he was only 11 years old. Neither had experienced death outside of the loss of a pet. All grandparents were still alive, along with aunts, uncles, and cousins. My two children are very different and had two very different reactions. I cannot even imagine what their initial internal feelings were, along with unasked questions that never came forth. Just thinking about it, my heart still hurts for them.

I had said my peace with Brad before his passing and knew that we would continue to have further connection after his death.

Brad's Celebration of Life

You wouldn't think celebrating someone's life would also bring a lot of judgment and opinions, but it certainly can—and did for me.

It was a bit of a whirlwind for the next several days. Family and friends were flying to Colorado for the memorial service. We did not want to do the service on Halloween and the kids were due back at school from fall break. Family was going to need to go back to their lives and the mortuary could provide what we needed on this time frame. So, we opted to have the service on October 30th.

I was lucky to have some amazing support. Many friends stepped in to help manage the service, make calls and even helped write the obituary. Jan, Maggie, Robin, Cindy and a host of others were front and center and helped wherever they could. Even Sophia's cousins, Chris and Mat, came to her aid in finding an outfit for the service and fed her olives—one of her favorite things. This helped her keep focused on the task at hand.

If people wanted to do something in honor of Brad, I asked them to donate to the National Association of Mental Illness (NAMI) instead of sending flowers if they wanted to do something in honor of Brad. Still, beautiful flowers and plants arrived, which I did appreciate.

My dear friend Jacqueline ordered a sympathy arrangement. Instead of the flowers she ordered, a dozen large red roses showed up at our home. Obviously, red roses are not your typical memorial flowers for a widow and her children, so they stood out. For years Brad would give me red roses. I always asked him to give me other flowers or colors but he rarely did. I really feel that this was Brad telling me from the other side that he still loved me, even if he did blame me before his crossing.

Both kids decided to speak at their father's celebration. I was amazed at their vulnerability and willingness to share feelings and happy memories of their dad. I chose not to speak at his service. I didn't want Brad's service to be about me, and I truly wanted to honor my in-laws and Brad's family. I hadn't spoken to them for about a year and they didn't know what was really going on. And naturally, they had a variety of reactions to what had just happened. Since I was closest to Brad and the situation, I felt that it was easier for them to blame me.

Painfully, I overheard many talking about the fact that Brad had sent an email to all the family members the morning of his death blaming me for his choice of suicide.

Not speaking seemed to make sense at this time. Jake and Sophia did a wonderful tribute to their father—sharing the good. I had said my peace with him before his passing and knew that we would continue to have further connection after his death.

The minister that agreed to do the eulogy was a friend and a lovely person. Both kids are baptized, even though we are not religious people—rather more spiritual. My family was in a separate room before the service and she came in and offered a prayer. Both my kids and I said a firm "NO." I am sure she wasn't expecting that, but it was what we wanted.

A piece of advice: The service is important for closure, honoring your loved one, and your healing process. If the service didn't go the way you hoped, or wasn't what you expected, remember that it doesn't have to look a certain way or be at a certain time. Even if you weren't invited because of family conflict, have your own ceremony to honor your loved one. Do what feels right for your heart and your own healing.

In addition to dealing with Brad's suicide and caring for my children, I also had to deal with inappropriate and offensive things that others said and did—and so may you.

My sister-in-law, Jane, who I spoke about earlier, walks into our home and loudly demands a stiff drink. She did not console her niece or nephew, her in-laws, or anyone else in the house. My mother-in-law then walks in and says, "You know this happened to Jane."

"What happened to her? Did her husband attempt suicide?" I asked.

What she was trying to say was that Jane had been suicidal at one point and that it could have been "her" deciding to take her own life. How words got flipped to make Brad's death about Jane, I don't know. What I do know is that Jane had no empathy for what had just happened. Sadly, she only thought of herself.

Jane also insisted on speaking at Brad's service, something that surprised several of us. She and Brad did not care for each other. I believe that she had a need to make it about herself to get attention. Her outline was long and very religious—something Brad would not have wanted. I let this slide. I believe these services are for the living and those who have crossed really don't have an opinion on what we do to honor them. Thank goodness my friend Jan convinced her to shorten the speech. She always found a way to make it about herself, and Brad's death was no exception.

When dealing with a suicide, many people will share all the details with everyone. I chose not to. It was interesting that all of a sudden former clients came to our home, deciding to push their way in. I had one individual corner me and demand to know everything. I also had someone corner my assistant, demanding to know all the details right in front of my in-laws who had just arrived. It was very awkward and certainly inappropriate. So many people do not know how to respond to a loss.

Even my very good friends who thought they were helping me in this situation crossed some very sensitive boundaries. I found out years later that they had "banned" students and clients from contacting me to give condolences.

My father-in-law and brother-in-law both had served in the Air Force and decided to wear their dress uniforms. I thought they looked perfect. And they both spoke about Brad in a positive way at the service. It surprised me when someone actually sought me out to say, "They 'should not' have worn their military uniforms." My take on this: This person "should" have kept her opinion to herself. I had no idea why she cared what Brad's father and brother wore for his service.

You may encounter unexpected comments like this also. At the service, I even had a guest mention that he thought it was odd that we had Brad's service so quickly. "Why was it planned so fast?" Seriously! Is this what goes through the minds of some people when someone dies? It felt as though they were implying I had been planning this for some time. WHAT?

Actually, Jan had managed many services and stepped in to make this easy on me. So why did a guest question this particular service?

After the service we had a dove release. And according to my father-in-law and brother-in-law, the flight pattern the bird flew was a technical maneuver. I am sure that Brad had something to do with that.

I felt at a loss trying to greet everyone and stay emotionally centered.

The Sheppards are loyal individuals who supported Brad in every way they could. The year before Brad's death was the only time they didn't communicate with me. After his passing, we reconnected and I was once again grateful for them. They were there for their son and that's where they needed to be. That was their way of supporting Brad and we knew after his death that he was reconnecting them with me.

I've always loved my father-in-law. I was and am grateful he is in our lives. He supported me from the first day I met him, including supporting my work as a medium. He would even invite friends over while I was visiting to have me "read" for them. Both my in-laws were wonderful to the kids.

It was surprising to me that during this ceremony some people pushed their way through the crowd and past my family to grab me during a moment of silence. Sometimes there are people who forget all proper boundaries in these situations.

I had great friends provide food to serve about 500 guests. These friends gave me unconditional support and touched my heart. I walked into the venue and people started lining up to give me their condolences. I had not planned on this; I was not prepared. But I felt that these guests wanted to acknowledge me, give me a hug, and tell me they were sorry for my loss. Many of whom I had not seen for years.

As I looked around, family members were talking and eating. I was standing alone in the midst of all of it. Catching the eye of my minister, I was hoping she would stand with me. Instead, she said, "This eulogy was the hardest thing I've ever done. I need a little time alone." I didn't know what to say, but I felt at a loss trying to greet everyone and stay emotionally centered.

I later heard that several people were surprised at my controlled state. They imagined I would be more upset. I couldn't seem to win! It wasn't a game; it was my life. And I was trying my best to navigate this devastating time.

After the Whirlwind

My home had become a little scary. I never knew who or what was on the other side of the door when I opened it. Prior clients would show up at my door wanting to help with my children. A neighbor that I was barely acquainted with told everyone what had happened without my permission and without asking how she could support my family in this difficult time. I was trying to keep my children protected, but people just do and say what they want and don't always feel the need to be kind.

A few weeks later, Jake went to this same neighbors' home to "hang out" with her children as a distraction. Her comment to Jake was "just get over it. My sister just died in a car accident and that just is what you have to do." She also let Jake play with a toy gun that he brought home. I never allowed my kids to play with guns, ever. It is not in my belief system.

Alarmed, I called her as I watched Jake hold the gun to his head and pull the trigger over and over again. I didn't want to make it a big deal in front of him. He didn't even know how Brad had died. On some level, I felt he was connecting with his father. When I asked her if she had given him the toy gun and she said "yes" with an attitude, I realized she didn't think it was significant. Well, it was to me.

Even at school other students would tell my kids that their dad was going to hell. Where is the compassion? Here we are dealing with this significant loss and people make it about them. They say things without thinking and feel they have to know details. It's like reading tabloids about people that can be very hurtful. Why do people believe this is okay?

There are a lot more incidents that occurred, but these are a few that I recalled. But then I thought to myself, do I share these or not? If it helps one person do the right thing or for those grieving to know that they are not alone, then it's good that I shared.

I'm hoping to help people learn how to support others and it's a reminder to not say or do stupid things while people are grieving. If these sort of things have happened to you, well, you're not alone.

6

The Gun

My question is where were my rights?
Where were my children's rights?

Brad and I had talked for years about purchasing a handgun for protection, but we always decided against it. After he died, I learned that he had purchased a gun a few months before his suicide.

I never saw the gun. The police took it after he died. From my understanding, he bought the gun at a pawn shop and I have no idea what the shop's guidelines were nor do I know where the gun ended up. The detectives never notified me as to what they did with it.

Brad wasn't in a good place mentally. I wish I would have been able to do something to help him. I believe that if any type of weapon is brought into a home where others live, the family or people within that residence have to agree upon having it there. With that being said, there are certainly a lot of other ways to die by suicide.

Brad was very definite about his suicide, and how can we predict the actions of a person who is depressed? How do we know what actions they will take? We can't and we don't. Things can change very quickly. I had no idea that he had bought a handgun where we had two young children in our home.

How can we predict the actions of a person who is depressed?

The topic of guns is very controversial these days, and I'm only coming at it from my one personal experience. I know without a doubt if I would have received a call, letter, or anything from a gun seller, I could have stopped him from his purchase. Where were my rights? Where were my children's rights?

7

Here We Go Again!

Sometimes we can manage them
(challenges and obstacles) and other times,
it feels as though it's too overwhelming
to take another breath.

Suicide never involves just one person. Those that are left behind are impacted. Some are filled with guilt; others are deeply hurt; and many are just bewildered.

> *How could this have happened?*
> *We had no idea he was so depressed.*
> *Why didn't she reach out to us?*
> *Why didn't his doctor let us know how desperate he was?*
> *Why didn't his boss tell me how frantic his behavior had become?*
> *Why did I not see how hopeless she felt everything was?*

Family and friends are at a loss. They can even turn against each other with finger pointing, snide and hurtful remarks—

even untruths. Yes, it's not uncommon to lose more than just the one from suicide.

During the summer of 2012, Sophia and her cousin Mat talked almost daily. Mat was going to propose to his girlfriend and Sophia was working with him on designing an engagement ring. He was living in Florida with his parents and seemed happy with life.

When his uncle Brad dies, he flew out with his family for the service. He approached me and shared how disappointed he was in his uncle. Mat told me "I want to make a difference". Brads death and his mom's brother in law who offered support and encouragement is why he decided to become a police officer— something he accomplished, and a career he loved. Brad and Mat shared a dry sense of humor and an intelligent mind.

Brad's suicide had rattled all of us in different ways. When Mat graduated from college with a bachelor's degree in Criminal Justice and walked summa cum laude from Grand Canyon University, all of us celebrated with him. As his Aunt, I was pleased that something positive was happening in our family.

Well, as life has it, we all face challenges and obstacles in our lives. Sometimes we can manage them. And other times, it feels as though it's too overwhelming to take another breath. Mat was no different.

Mat followed my husband's path.

We are not entirely sure of the circumstances or what actually took place. All we know is there was some kind of situation that became elevated and Mat followed my husband's path four years later almost to the day of his Uncle Brad's suicide. Brad died October 27, 2008, and his memorial service was October 30. Mat died October 30, 2012. Whether the anniversary of Brad's death influenced Mat, I don't know. I do know that since his death, I feel Mat around often and know he is at peace.

During this time, I had my own physical challenges. The week before Mat died, I had been in ICU for four days with pneumonia. Still weak, my mother came out to help in my recovery when I received the call about Mat. Sophia was in Rhode Island attending school. I immediately called, telling her of her cousin's suicide. Sophia was shocked, as was my 15-year-old son Jake.

Being the oldest grandchild on the Sheppard side of the family, Mat's death was another huge impact to my family. We were in disbelief that another family member had taken his life. We flew to Florida to support Mat's family, their community and to be with my brother and sister-in-law. Along with my children, my companion that followed me everywhere was my oxygen tank—a constant reminder to me at the time of just how frail we all could be.

The military has great meaning to us and is woven throughout our family history. Mat's father was a retired Air Force Colonel and his Uncle Brad's father was a retired Major General Air Force Commander. I'm sure the challenges for the families' healing was not an easy one. The life of anyone in the military is to be of service with strong minds that support others in that type of life. The topic of suicide wasn't an open one—more like a buried taboo.

Everyone deals with their losses in their own way and this family and mine were no exception. Mat's mother, my sister in-law, has never really warmed-up to me, even though both her sons were frequent visitors to my home and communicated often with my kids. One time while she and her children were visiting, she was bold enough to tell me that she really didn't like me. I just laughed and said, "Yah, I know." It was always a struggle to play nice together. My choice in dealing with her was to just keep my mouth shut and have a few adult beverages. As the saying goes: You can't choose your family.

Prior to flying down for Mat's services, a friend helped me make a small photo album of him over the years during family visits. I also brought my *Forever Connected* Oracle Cards. I wanted to be positive for them or anyone who was interested in how I used them. Her sisters and I, with my oxygen tank in tow, went shopping to buy food and other items to help out while we were all in town.

I wasn't expecting a hug or even a thank you given our track record and the fact her son had just died. But, what I didn't expect was for her to throw the album with the memories our family had accumulated and cards across the table when I presented them to her. "I don't want to see any of this stuff," she said, almost with venom in her voice.

Friends and family may distance themselves, point fingers, or turn things around during these times.

Whether the others told her that I had purchased all the food —spending several hundred dollars—I don't know. What I do know is that she became very upset that I took some cookies that I purchased back to the hotel for a snack and she accused me of stealing food from her. I couldn't win!

The afternoon before we returned home, she showed pictures of Mat's police graduation. None of us had seen them and we began to share stories about Mat as a kid and young adult. And still, she refused to acknowledge me, much less look at the small album I gave her. We all grieved for and with her. And we grieved for the loss of a fine young man who had great promise, still not understanding why he did it. It could be that possibly she felt that my husband was to blame because he took his life.

Maybe I was the indirect target for her anger. I don't know what was going on in her mind. I do know that from a medium's perspective and from feeling his presence, Mat is at peace and bares no anger toward me.

When she and I had a moment to talk, I shared that I had been worried about another suicide in our family for some time —since Brad's death four years earlier. Never had I imagined it would have been Mat. With all the kids and extended family, I worried about all of them, but it didn't cross my mind that Mat would make this choice.

What I found out later, is she told people I said I was glad it was Mat and not my son Jake. Obviously, I was upset—even angry—that she would tell others this outrageous statement and anyone would believe her. It hurt my heart that she turned something around that was meant for us to discuss the issue of suicide. *How could I ever be happy about anyone dying?*

Although I have no communication with her today, I am in contact with my nephew Chris, Mat's younger brother. My family has been honored to participate in Chris's life and promised him that we would stay in closer contact since Mat's death. We are so proud of him; he is on his way to becoming a psychologist. With these traumatic experiences, we believe he will be amazing at helping so many people.

I've gone back and forth about including Mat's story in this book. My intention is to share how everyone deals with loss and how we can hurt others that are grieving as well. When someone dies from suicide, we lose more family than just the one from the suicide.

Remember this: Friends and family may distance themselves, point fingers, or twist things around during these times. Just don't be surprised at what evolves. What is normal in the array of emotions and reactions when death occurs? Their truth: Their reaction is "normal" for what has happened.

I wish for healing for Mat's family. My job is to respect what they need and not what I want. People grieve differently and I will not force my way into anyone else's life. I think that's an important concept for all of us to grasp.

There is more to our family dynamics and relationships, just as you have in yours. My intention is to share that after a significant loss of any kind, many things change in the dynamics of relationships. Some that were close and solid may become frail. And some that were already fragile or estranged can become more so or strengthened.

My family experienced suicide twice within a four-year period. Something we never contemplated happening to us. Those kind of things happen to other people, not us. But, it did.

The reality is you can't prepare, but being aware can help with managing life. It is imperative that you breathe, love, and move forward once again.

8

Doing the Best That I Can

*I may have more tools,
but it does not stop me from being human.*

One of the many things I have realized through this time of writing and reflecting, is I still had more lessons to learn before I could share my story. I have had to share some things that are difficult and sometimes still very raw.

As a medium I understand grief, death, and healing because my profession is about helping others through this process. It didn't come as easily when the loss was my own. I may have more tools, but it doesn't stop me from being human.

My intentions are to provide another insight to those of you who like me grieve from losses of mental illness and suicide. I wanted to put my words on paper … to create a book with the idea of helping others along their path to healing.

Initially, I struggled with the grief that was my partner in my writing, reminiscing about the past as I tried to heal in the present. This was a lot to ask of myself. But, as I want to share with you, my answer for all of this is honest and simply stated. I am doing the best that I can for where I am today.

I was resistant to questions about my writing and truly didn't know why.

I was asked often: How far along are you? How can I help? When are you going to be done with your book? It became overwhelming.

There were times when I was very committed to completing my thoughts on paper. I even tried to lock myself away somewhere quiet to dedicate time to my writing. Telling my story was just such a struggle to complete. I could be very hard on myself, but I also tried to trust my process and timing, realizing they may be different than that of the Universal plan.

I know that my journey of healing is far from over, but I do know I'm stronger than I imagined.

9

All Children Cope Differently

My best advice is there is no one way
of helping your children through a significant loss.
And how you handle it will be up to you.

I believe that there should be no criticism of how people handle grief. Sophia and Jake processed theirs very differently. Sophia decided on distraction, concentrating on getting through school early. She doubled up on her classes, never taking a break, choosing to work through the summers and kept very busy, doing as much as she could. She graduated from high school early and college as well. She earned her bachelor's degree in two years—walking magna cum laude! I was one proud mom!

Jake took a different path. He became very sad and struggled in his own way. School became more difficult and he cried every night at bedtime and every morning when I dropped him off at school. These were the times when I became angrier with Brad's choice. How could he do this to our kids? The pain he caused our children was felt deeply. However, I also know that he truly believed he was causing more pain being alive than being dead.

I understood it, I just didn't like it. We never have to like it. What we have to learn is to come to terms with it. I did.

Eventually, I was able to place Jake in another school with the help of a dear friend who was a counselor. The school he had been attending was wonderful and they were amazingly supportive of Jake's needs. But the new school had very small class sizes and provided a unique program that was a perfect fit for him. This is when things became better for Jake. His attitude improved; his grades improved. He liked his school and eventually became the captain of the basketball team. He received many awards and I could see his enhanced self-esteem. My Jake was back!

Sophia chose not to attend any counseling or grief groups, however, Jake did. I was so proud of him to be willing to put himself in those environments. For two summers, he attended the Camp Comfort Bereavement Camp for Kids in Evergreen, Colorado, part of Camp Comfort–Mount Evans. This was a wonderful experience for him and I continue to support the organization. A weekend designed for children under a particular age, matching each camper with an adult buddy who has been trained to help. The camp's intention is to show kids that they are not alone, that there are others who have experienced losses similar to theirs. The adult buddies show them ways to grieve and ways to still be a kid.

The second year he attended, they asked him to speak on the last day of the camp when all the families came to celebrate their loved ones who had died and to take home their children. Jake rocked that afternoon and everyone in attendance was impressed.

As his mom, I was so proud and, of course, the tears ran down my face at Jake's brave soul, sharing his story and his experiences at Camp Comfort to this large bereaved audience of kids and adults. When he jumped into the car for the ride home, he was smiling from ear-to-ear.

A new Jake surfaced. He asked if he could emcee my classes that I held for the public once a month. His father used to do this, and Jake wanted to step into his shoes. I was witnessing his healing.

Both Brad's and my nephew Mat's names are placed on bricks at the Camp Comfort park. It would be wonderful to see many more organizations such as this one. They are a testament to helping children and families with their grief.

Another organization that Jake attended was Judi's House in Denver, Colorado, founded by former NFL quarterback Brian Griese and his wife, Dr. Brook Griese, a clinical psychologist specializing in childhood trauma and loss. It is devoted exclusively to supporting grieving children and their families.

Brian's mother died of cancer when he was 11. When he became an NFL player, he wanted to give back to children that had been through similar situations. Judi's House has helped thousands.

During this time, Jake still didn't want to know how his father had died. Once, he "sort of" asked Sophia. Her response, "He died of a broken heart." Jake didn't want to know more. Even though I was being advised to tell Jake what happened, I still didn't feel as if I was supposed to yet. So, I didn't.

At one of my sessions, children kept coming through during her session that she couldn't recognize. We realized the spirits were those of her patients who had passed. When the reading was complete, I asked her if I could ask a professional question. **Everyone has his or her personal way of grieving.** I felt I could trust what she said without hesitation. I shared with her that I had not told Jake about how his father had died, and he had never asked. Was this the right thing to do?

Her advice was crystal clear. "Jake is telling you he doesn't want to know. He is letting you know how he wants to grieve, and you should respect it." So, I continued with what Jake was requesting. When he was ready, he would let Sophia or me know.

The kids have always been very close and when Jake needs to talk, he goes to Sophia the most often. I assume that has put pressure on her, but she handles it well with no complaints. I'm glad they support each other in so many ways. One day, he began asking her questions. Eventually, he figured it out, in his own way and on his own timetable. It's what my son needed and I'm grateful that I was able to honor that for him.

Please remember: Everyone has his or her personal way of grieving. Respect that process. It is important for each individual's healing.

Remembering Their Dad

To this day, we still talk about their dad. As time has passed, I share more about him in ways that let them know he is still a big part of their lives. I also feel as if I can share with my own healing heart. It is helpful to remind myself—my heart—that we did have a great love and we brought two amazing children into this world.

I knew many ways to remember their father. Since Brad had been the emcee, we had his voice on CDs from the classes we recorded. My producer and dear friend, Mike Willson, took Brad's voice off of the CDs and added the song "Yesterday" by the Beatles on one CD for us to have. It was and is a wonderful way to hear his voice again. As the kids grew, I knew there would be times they would want to hear his voice. Even perhaps for their children to hear—just to think of him. I've listened a few times and it is certainly difficult to hear, but also very healing, especially hearing his sense of humor. Brad was a great public speaker and carried a strong voice with great intention. I do miss that, the old Brad I married.

My friends and clients, Disa and Bill Van Orman, have a business that helps with grief. They take molds which can be for art and or remembrance. It is quite an amazing process. When Brad died, I reached out to Disa and asked if she could go to the mortuary and do a mold of Brad's hands. Some may think this is odd or even morbid, but Jan would tell me that after her father had passed, she always missed his hands—holding them and looking at them. Since I only had this one chance to get his hands molded, I did it. Later, we decided to all have our hands done so we could have this connection. I'm not sure if they will ever want either the CDs or the molded hands, but I have them. What we did notice is that Jake's hands look much like his father's. I'm not sure we would have known that if we didn't have them done.

I also had my friend, Diana Fox, make two quilts out of some of his shirts. She added pictures of them with their dad. During the making of this quilt, their cousin Mat suicided. I had her add a picture of them with Mat to the quilt as well. I'm not sure they have used them much at this point. Perhaps they will be valuable to them in later years.

Brad loved watches and had several. Four years after his passing, I was able to let the kids go through his collection and decide what they wanted to keep and what they wanted to give to other family members. Because they had been so young, I chose to wait until they were older before deciding what they wanted to do with their father's things.

When Brad's mother passed from heart failure while taking a nap, Jake and Sophia had just arrived in Europe. The family all agreed that it was best that they enjoy their European vacation rather than fly back for her funeral. They had already planned to spread some of Brad's ashes in Vicenza, which was where he had some of his favorite memories from childhood as a military family.

I decided to send some of her ashes to them, so they could release them with Brad's. They found the home that the Sheppards had lived in while in Vicenza. In a park nearby, they released Brad's and a bit of their grandmother's ashes. When they arrived in the favorite city of their grandmother, they released the rest of her ashes. This was their way of honoring both their dad and grandmother.

My best advice is there is no one way of helping your children through a significant loss. How you handle it will be up to you. Some things I share that worked for me may be useful to you. But keep in mind, each child is different, and each death is unique. Do what your gut tells you and trust it.

The Eye
of the Storm

When individuals are in the eye of their storm,
they begin to feel the veil that is peaceful and allows them
to gain energy and leave their human body.

Hurricanes and suicides have similarities. Hurricanes gather and grow in power when a series of climate events come together that in turn can create a destructive force that causes devastation before it subsides, often having immeasurable consequences for those affected. In addition, the center or "eye" of the storm is often calm and quiet, almost eerily so.

An impending suicide may be seeded in a distance, and builds with a series of what, at first glance, appears seemingly insignificant events and/or behaviors. Individually, an event or behavior neither seems alarming nor has little effect. Collectively, though, they can build, resulting in a release of destructive force that causes devastation often with immeasurable consequences for those affected. And sometimes just when you think the worst has passed and things are getting better, you realize it was just the calm before the storm.

When anyone first hears the words that a loved one has died by suicide, shock is the common reaction. Even if the loved one was not in a healthy state. Addiction could have been the genesis, or a diagnosis of mental illness such as bipolar disease or a traumatic event that leads to PTSD. Maybe your loved one seemed lost and was not accepting guidance or any support when his/her job or relationship ended unexpectedly. The news that suicide has occurred is NOT expected. You and others around you are dumbfounded —shocked that this person could have taken his/her own life.

You and others around you are dumbfounded.

When we are concerned about someone we love, we are always hopeful they will seek help and find their direction once again. If you have tried desperately without success to help, you may replay these thoughts over and over again. You ask:

Could I have done more?
Did I miss something?
Did I do something to upset him/her?
Should I have known the last time
we talked that he/she was so desperate?

The question of WHY is in every thought we have when we begin to dissect the reality that our loved one has suicided. It is not uncommon to recall every word, action, and emotion we had about this loved one after his/her death. The result? We end up beating ourselves up for not doing one more thing we believed may have kept this person from dying.

For those that had no idea and are thus shocked because they didn't realize the pain a person was experiencing, guilt permeates their thoughts. They are disappointed that the person never reached out to ask for help, believing that if a connection had been made, the suicide could have been prevented.

It is not unusual to question your actions and those of the suicide victim without getting any resolution. Even knowing that perhaps there was nothing anyone could have done to stop the suicide. It can still leave you unsettled. It's always difficult to accept the fact that it has happened. You may even become angry because he or she did not reach out to you, knowing that you would have done anything to help.

What if you tried to help multiple times with the same results? And you know that you became angry with him/her. Did you decide at one point to stop supporting this person because it was going nowhere? Were you hoping that tough love would make the difference? But it didn't, and now guilt may weigh heavily on your heart, believing you abandoned this person and that's why he/she gave up and chose to die by suicide.

For some, it seems as if the suicide victims are in the eye of the storm.

I've worked with thousands of clients who have lost someone from suicide, and no matter what their story is with their mother, father, grandparent, spouse, child, sibling, best friend and so on, it's always the same. They want to know "why." Why did this happen? Could they have done something differently? Are they okay now?

For some, it seems as if the suicide victims are in the eye of the storm. You may even reflect back, remembering that this person had become calm for the first time in weeks, months, or even years. You may even have believed that he/she was so much better. And that things were going to be all right. An example of this comes from clients that work in hospice who tell me that when someone is ready to die, it takes energy for the final process to occur.

You may have experienced this with someone dying of cancer or another illness. After many days in hospice, you are waiting for him/her to make the transition. You and your family stay around the clock, never leaving your loved without someone there. It's a 24-hour vigil. As the day or evening progresses, you may notice that he or she becomes more awake, even talking and perhaps a smile appears on dying person's face. Everyone takes a moment and relaxes. The family decides to breathe, grab a bite to eat, take a shower or a nap, and that's when the transition takes place.

You are surprised. You wonder why you didn't stay longer or know death was imminent. Please understand this: It takes energy to come into this world; and it takes energy to leave it.

Individuals who feel that life is too complicated, and their world is spinning around them, may sense that they have no control to change the situation of their life, or how they feel about themselves. Their mind makes them believe that everything is wrong and there are no positive solutions. Even if they are helped and supported by friends, family, therapy, and medications, they believe there is no relief from their pain, which is very real to them. For them, life has become one that is not worth living.

It takes energy to come into this world; and it takes energy to leave it.

When individuals are in the eye of their storm, they begin to feel the veil that is peaceful and allows them to gain energy and leave their human body. The veil is what separates us from our earth existence and our human selves and the spirit world. Humans have many ways of understanding or providing a name of the spirit world—heaven, the other side, the veil.

While sharing with others that have had a loved one die from suicide, it may be very similar or not at all the same. Just as with any loss or birth, it has its own unique path.

One thing that appears consistent in the grief and process after a suicide is thinking you didn't know the person was so sad because he or she didn't act depressed. Actually, you may have remembered the person seemingly very upbeat, a common theme for many who have experienced a person's death from suicide.

11

Are There Answers to Your Questions?

You are not defeated
nor have you done anything wrong.

Whatever your situation is that has brought you to this book, my heart goes out to you. You are looking for answers to your questions about the pain you incurred—whether it was from some trauma, an accident, a death, suicide or any other type of loss. What you are going through is a journey. It can feel lonely and very isolating.

I have found that when there is death by suicide, few understand how unique it is to all other deaths. Those left behind to heal have emotions that can extend in a variety of ways and it can take years to heal. Too many times, it lingers, never freeing those left behind. My personal experience and those of the many thousands I've worked with have shown me that it is possible to understand and collect new insights. Insights that will *help to heal your heart*, forgive *your loved one*, and *forgive yourself.*

When death occurs to someone close to you from an accident or illness, it can have a tragic cloud around it. You may begin to question and challenge your personal beliefs. Is there a God? Is there an afterlife? What is it like on the other side? Do they see us? Is there a heaven or hell? And so on.

However, when experiencing a loss from suicide, for most, the process for recovering from this particular tragedy seems far more challenging. Guilt and regret seem to be on the top of the emotional roller coaster ride.

When experiencing a loss from suicide, for most, the process for recovering from this particular tragedy seems far more challenging.

Even if you are someone who has done a lot of work, including reading books, going to therapy, participating in support groups, and working with a spiritual counselor, you may still feel at a loss. My questions for you become:

Do you still feel that things are unresolved?
Do you still have unanswered questions,
no matter what work you have done?
Do you continue to feel the deep pain with many regrets?

Not in my wildest dreams would I ever have imagined I would be writing a book that talks about suicide. But, you probably never imagined you would be reading a book that talks about suicide and for that reason, I'm deeply sorry.

My intention in talking about this subject in *Grieving to Believing* is to share my:

• personal experiences with loved ones;

• insights and the work that I've done for almost two decades as a medium;

- spiritual beliefs as well as the psychological point of view that suicide is a disease;

- personal experiences for what I believe happens to those who die from suicide;

- insights as a journey to suicide begins; and perspectives about healing and self-forgiveness, while also learning to connect with those who have passed.

- Change the stigma and verbiage related to suicide. The correct terms are "died by suicide" or "suicided". They did not "commit" a crime. There was mental illness involved.

You will learn how to manage those in your community who are judgmental of you or what others "believe" happened. Some may feel suicide is contagious or it's a sin and may abandon you. The emotions and rejections can show up in so many unexpected ways. Not only are you trying to manage your healing, you may also be dealing with surprised reactions from what you thought was your support system.

There will be times you just want to close your door and sit in the dark. I do understand because there were times I felt like that. But, making any effort will provide one more of the pieces to the puzzle called healing. I always recommend that you join support groups, talk to your

Not one book, one therapy session, or one thing will provide the healing needed.

clergyman, friends, family, and a therapist—individuals you feel will listen and not try to "fix" or judge you.

Please understand this: *You have not done anything wrong.* Someone you love died by suicide. People die by suicide because they have an illness, just like any other type of disease. I tell people when I am asked about the way I understand suicide is that it's a cancer of the mind. Remember, it's an illness and people die when they are very ill.

When you experience loss from a suicide, you will have it near your heart and mind from the moment of your awareness that your loved one is gone until you are no longer here. For many, it is one loss that is difficult to comprehend. It doesn't matter if you are in the beginning stages of your healing or you have been in the process for many years, you may never feel as if it will have an ending.

Of course, you never imagined this would be one of your life's experiences. It can take many tools to help in the healing for yourself and those in your life. If you are at the beginning of this process, this book just scratched the surface. Not one book, one therapy session, or one thing will provide all of the healing needed. One of the best pieces of advice I can give you is to take "your" time—the time that you need and the steps that work best for you. Find your courage and understand more about this terrible disease. When you do, you can find your way on your journey of healing.

Sometimes we are put into situations that we do not expect, as I was when my husband chose to die by suicide. Through this journey I've been able to understand and help support those that have either had a session to connect with their loved one or those that may have contemplated suicide but have made another choice—to begin to heal and find a way to continue being with us.

Through this process, even with all of the information you have received regarding suicide, you may continue to have more questions than answers. It's common. My personal goal is to provide at least one more nugget in your journey of healing. I am grateful to many people who've lost loved ones from suicide who chose to help me along my path.

12

Guilt

*Many of us feel guilty for so many things
that we have said or done.*

I have found that most of us don't deal well with the dying process and death—at least in the United States. But maybe your profession or your belief system has helped you, or the example of others has provided you with tools. However, most of us skirt around or ignore the topic, considering it too sensitive and depressing. Religion can also be a factor so it's not often a topic for discussion.

It's a mistake and one that can have a domino consequence to it.

When your personal tool box in dealing with death is empty, it limits the process of grief along with how to handle any guilt. It plays heavy on your heart and mind causing anxiety. We may not trust ourselves and may not believe we deserve good things. This doesn't mean that you can't learn to manage guilt with new insights. Many feel guilty and regret so many things that they have said or done. Some carry these transgressions—no matter how big or small—for years. The mere memory can create massive amounts of guilt and grief that could have been dealt with years earlier.

Religion, family, friends and the community have created rules for what they believe is right or wrong. If anyone steps beyond those rules, it becomes fairly easy for others to point fingers and judge. This conditioning can last a lifetime, affecting how you feel … even making you feel that you don't deserve much of anything. Any joy in living is dampened.

If your loved one died at the hands of another, whether accidental or intentional, society has put laws in place that punish the perpetrator. You may still feel a huge amount of guilt that you were not able to protect your loved one. You and your community should be safe and protected from those who purposefully injure another. Not that every time we are able to prosecute a perpetrator, but we have a society that wants good people to be protected.

If you currently deal with guilt-related issues, then it can increase your grief even more.

When it comes to innocent hurts to someone, such as a lie about not being able to attend a gathering or perhaps you lied that you didn't receive person's text, they may be considered less judgmentally. But many will carry the burden of guilt. This isn't about whether these patterns are acceptable or not, rather it's about your moral code and how you feel you want to live your life.

If you're always feeling guilty, then healing from your loved one's passing may be a lot to manage, especially if it was a suicide. You may feel guilty for having someone else in your life. You may feel guilty when you can't give back as much as another person can. You may even feel guilty about not returning phone calls or remembering someone's birthday. Feeling guilty is something you may encounter often—most do. In fact, it may be a constant stream of thoughts of guilt that you end up punishing yourself because of it.

For others, guilt may not even be in their vocabulary, so they will not understand what you are talking about. This doesn't mean that either of you are grieving the wrong way. It may be how grief is perceived or it's simply a form of belief and a different code of ethics. We can even review how some religions have codes that can create guilt for "things" where a different religion would be accepting of these "things." It's a matter of what you have been taught, shown, and experienced that forms your standards to manage guilt. Many are programmed to feel guilt.

Guilt can certainly be a part of most of our grief, no matter how someone we love dies. On the topic of suicide, it seems to be at the forefront. People can sometimes point fingers at others thinking they "should" have done something to prevent the suicide. Guilt doesn't change what happened.

There are a few ways to look at the sadness of suicide. Sometimes our own guilt refers to the choices they made so they believe suicide is their only option. Some may feel peer pressure or judgment from others, and believe that suicide is what others would want for them. In some circumstances, an illness or financial loss can be their reasoning for suicide.

Mental illness, grief, or a feeling that there are no options left after maybe a job loss or financial disaster pressures them into thinking that suicide is their solution … and the only solution. Individuals who choose suicide may think that this is what's best for them to escape their circumstance or life issue. And if you knew that happened to someone you were connected with, you may think, if only I had known …

I used to believe that no one can force someone into suicide, just like no one forces cancer, Alzheimer's, or an accident on a person … resulting in a death. People will eventually die and we can' t stop it. When fingers are pointed or if you are feeling responsible for someone' s choice, know that you don't have that kind of power. It's what I used to believe. In recent years, things have been taking place that have changed my belief.

Young teenagers are now suiciding in groups, making agreements to all die on a chosen weekend. Recently there has been a social media game called The Blue Whale Challenge. It dares kids to do "tasks" eventually leading the player to take his or her young life. In fact, others who are in on "the game" encourage the player to "do it." And if you knew that happened to someone you were connected with, you may think, if only I had known …

Today, we have a mass epidemic of opioids, heroin, crack, and other drugs, which have caused death rates so high that some communities are unable to keep up with the bodies that arrive daily at the morgues. Some professionals refer to this as accidental suicide. This addiction doesn't limit the demographics from economic conditions, religion, education, or zip code. What do we do as a community and a country to address this? Many families are unaware of the drug/s a loved one is consuming. Once again, guilt comes into play. And if you knew that happened to someone you were connected with, you may think, if only I had known …

In my experience, I have never done a reading where some-one who died from suicide blamed anyone for his or her death. Even though my husband left notes to family members and myself that it was my fault, after his death he has never made me feel that I was to blame.

Before he passed, I begged him to talk to a doctor, get help, and take medications—but without success. Brad believed I was causing him unnecessary pain and if I would just change and let him do whatever he wanted, then he would be fine. Everything would be fine. The choices he was making were not acceptable and he couldn't see it. Nothing was fine. I know when I've been in a depressive state, it was so difficult to see things clearly. And many times I would jump to conclusions, which were most likely not accurate.

Women who have postpartum depression, or those suffering with PTSD or CTE can relate to how the world looks and feels different than it once was. They are not trying to do anything wrong, it's only that their state of mind has changed. Things become twisted—their reality becomes removed from the real, "normal" world.

We can't be responsible for someone's health. We can be supportive, understanding and patient. We can offer guidance and present possible solutions. It's up to that person to seek professional guidance and take the steps for healing.

What if you didn't know your loved one was depressed—he or she was a master of secrets and kept things from you. Maybe you just didn't have the "tools" to recognize that the behaviors, actions, and words being used were red flags of trouble ahead. When this happens, guilt can be a strong emotion. You're questioning yourself—thinking that you "should" have known. Or why didn't your best friend share his or her pain with you? Remember, all of us keep things from those we love. Boundaries could have been imposed, unbeknownst to you. Many people are ashamed to talk about their struggles and fears.

My years of experience reflect that the majority of men are less willing to share or seek help. This makes sense in our society because we have taught our little boys not to cry, to be strong, and even say to them, "Don't act like a little girl." So, of course, this upbringing isn't going to help men realize that it is okay to ask for help, and it's not a sign that they are not strong. If we can help our communities understand that mental illness should not to be seen as shameful or a weakness, but rather a disease, perhaps they can ask for help. We then may see fewer suicides.

When we educate ourselves as a community about these things, then we can be more accepting of the paths of others. We don't have to experience it to understand it. I don't have to have breast cancer to be compassionate toward a friend with breast cancer. I can learn about the disease and help support that person in my life who is fighting the battle.

Guilt or pointing fingers doesn't resolve the issue of suicide. Sometimes it can even cause more suicides. I have seen that with clients who carried so much guilt from their loved one's passing that they followed the same course. How does this help anyone?

Guilt will always be a portion of the healing process when a loved one has died.

Instead, become educated on the topic, join support groups, raise awareness, and seek guidance. Suicide came into your life so now learn everything you can on the subject.

If you are blaming someone for your loved one's suicide, I encourage you to stop immediately. Learn to change your thinking. We all have free will. The individual made a terrible choice and we don't have to like it, agree with it, or support it. It's about our healing and awareness of this disease.

Guilt will always be a portion of the healing process when a loved one has died. This subject is something many will work on the most during their healing process.

13

Forgiveness Is Part of the Grieving Process

You can never control
what another person will do.

When you are grieving the loss by suicide, forgiveness has multiple layers: forgiving your loved one; forgiving yourself; and forgiving others.

It is truly amazing how many people will want to project the blame on someone when a loved one has suicided. I didn't realize the depth of Brad's mental illness. Not until after I had time to process and continue my healing, did I realize that he blamed me for his problems. But then I had to remind myself that was his state of mind at the time. He didn't want to seek help or accept he was depressed. It was far easier to blame the person who was closest to him—his wife.

Millions of couples divorce yearly, yet the choice of suicide as an end to their misery isn't considered. People lose jobs, struggle with their health, suffer from abuse, and so many other tough circumstances but they do not decide that suicide is the answer.

How many times have you been hurt and didn't decide to take your life, even consider it as an option? Even if you had seriously considered suicide, you didn't do it.

Understanding that suicide is an illness will help your healing. Over the years that I've worked with people, many have shared that they stayed in their marriages because they worried their partner would suicide. These partners are in need of medical attention. Staying with partners because there is a possibility that they may take their life isn't healthy. I don't want you to think setting boundaries is a way out of responsibilities you may have, but we simply don't have that kind of power to stop another human-being from his or her free will.

A close friend of mine was having dinner with another colleague and she shared her situation. She was divorcing and she was struggling because she was very worried about what her husband might do. She revealed that he was unstable and was concerned he would choose to suicide because he wasn't able to see his own issue of depression. The colleague was quiet for a few minutes after listening to the story and bluntly said, "You're just not that important." My friend was taken back and thought, *wow that's a little insensitive.* Then she continued, "You don't have the power to keep someone from doing whatever he or she wants."

With loved ones, you can support them on so many levels, "IF" they welcome it and believe they need help.

She is right. None of us has that kind of power and we shouldn't want anyone to feel he or she is responsible for our happiness. You can only participate the way you know and allow others to find their inner strength.

You get to decide how you want to think, believe, and respond to circumstances in your life. Even if you're the parent, you cannot make your children do what you think is best for them. This doesn't mean you give up or walk away. With loved ones, you can support them on so many levels, "IF" they welcome it and believe they need help.

You can do a lot, but you can't make them better.

Denial is common. If someone you care about is in denial that is his or her choice. You can do a lot, but you can't make him or her better. It is a personal choice.

People don't like to be told that they need to make a change. Some of us may desire change, but to be told that our lives depend on it isn't an easy thing to accept. Be it money, work, addictions, spiritual beliefs, or anything else that we fragile humans can experience, resistance rears its head.

DENIAL can be anyone's best friend, joined at the hip until denial isn't working any longer. Ideally, you want your loved one to step up and accept the changes that will be in his best interest. He has to see it for himself to make that choice. Otherwise, healing may not ever be reached.

When anyone, including you, feels depressed, it's normal to think those feelings are normal. It isn't until you feel healthy and have the energy to see yourself as others had seen you that you realize how distorted the old reality was. It's just how this disease works.

Have you ever known someone with an eating disorder? Karen and Richard Carpenter were a brother and sister singing sensation during the '70s. Karen saw a photo of herself as a chubby teen that prompted her to take action. She hired a personal trainer to trim down so she would "look better" on the stage. Bulking up wasn't what she wanted, but what she got after a few months. Karen fired the trainer and took measures into her own hands and quickly lost 20 pounds. She felt fabulous. Her friends agreed.

This seeded her anorexia nervosa, the eating disorder that eventually triggered heart failure and took her life when she was only 32. Carpenter's fans were shocked when her evolving skeleton shape was revealed in evening gowns. Rumors spread that she might have breast cancer. In the '70s, eating disorders weren't talked about, nor were they labeled as a form of mental illness. Her death in 1983 brought anorexia and other eating disorders out of the shadows.

People dealing with eating disorders see themselves as overweight, even obese, when everyone else clearly sees the opposite. Their minds believe this. Often, the consequences are tragic as they battle against this mental illness.

We all have situations that can provoke us to places that we didn't even realize we could land in. Our "logical" human self would instantly claim: *No way, I would never do that*. We are all vulnerable at times. When something is said or done to you at the wrong time or the wrong place, something inside of you can spiral to a place you never knew existed. The result: You can feel alone and think that no one else in the entire world feels like you.

You can manage your own healing and insight, but not that of another.

Forgiving Them and Yourself

There will be countless times when you think, even say out loud to yourself and others:

Why didn't he just ask for help?
Why didn't I answer the phone when she kept calling?
Why did I let her call go to voice mail?
Why didn't I take the time to go see him?

Whatever your experience was, you *may* have been able to help "that" day, but take a step back. You can never control what another person will do—never. If you were able to stop your loved one "that" time, but the individual didn't choose to receive therapy, take the prescribed medication, or whatever was needed to manage the depression, the waiting game continues. This is a "game" you did not realize was in play—a constant waiting game of when and how this person will make a terrible decision.

This may not be across the board in every situation, but you do not have the power you believe you do. You can manage your own healing and insight, but not that of another. Even in the most successful facilities that help with addictions, they can't prevent anyone from making a painful choice.

When you can take a deep look at an illness and understand that you can't prevent someone from dying from any disease, you will understand that mental illness isn't any different. By educating our world and changing the way we see this illness as a weakness, then we can begin preventing it. Unfortunately, because there is such judgment around the disease of mental illness, we haven't been able to truly help those suffering from it.

If we see someone in a wheel chair, blind, or a person with Down syndrome, we have compassion and can provide assistance to that person. Depression looks very different from physical illnesses, aliments, and handicaps that are observable and most don't provide the same compassion and support to those suffering from it. With this said, when someone is diagnosed with cancer and we can't see it with our eyes, we accept it because test results give us this information.

If someone doesn't get a diagnosis of mental illness from a medical professional, then it doesn't receive the attention or the respect it deserves. There is no understanding as to how to help someone, including ourselves with the illness. People are ashamed of the mental illness stigma, believing they will be judged. They may think that they did something wrong to have their mind turn on them. Then there will be those people who believe that they should be able to easily just change the way they think, and this nightmare will go away. I'm sure those with other diseases may also feel the same way: If I could just change the way I think, this will go away.

Now, I do believe in the power of positive thinking. We can heal in many ways by the way we live, eat, think and by our personal happiness. However, we are spiritual beings living a human life, which means we also have a body that responds to earthly experiences.

Forgiveness isn't easy in any situation. Be aware that even if you ask for it, someone may choose not to forgive you.

Having the spiritual aspect is also vital to our well-being. The relationship between the **mind, body,** and **spirit** is something we cannot ignore. Our mind and body are the physical pieces that are necessary for well-being. We can't ignore them. And our mind and body require a lot to stay healthy for our spirit to manifest into what we truly desire in our life.

Questions surface: Have you thought about depression? Have you thought about mental illness and the effects it can have on you or someone you love?

Do you believe mental illness and depression are curable?
Are mental illness and depression manageable?
How do you feel about using medications?
How do you feel about seeing a therapist to look deeply
into your past and what the triggers are?

If you believe that someone is "making it up" or "pretending" how they feel and they "should" just get over it, then healing and forgiveness will be a long battle. This is a disease. My opinion is this: Take it seriously as an illness and respect it as one.

Forgiveness isn't easy in any situation. Be aware that even if you ask for it, someone may choose not to forgive you. It's a challenge. While looking back on your life, have there been times that you have regretted saying something or doing something that hurt someone you cared about? I can answer that for you: Of course, you have—we all have. If we could take it back, we certainly would.

People have done the same to you—saying and doing things that they regret now hangs on whatever occurred. If you can forgive them and **We are all learning and sometimes it's a slow process.** learn to begin to forgive yourself, then the healing begins. While looking back at my life, there are so many times that I have regretted the choices I have made, knowing I hurt others and they probably haven't forgiven me.

The only thing I can do at this point, is learn from these experiences. One of my sayings is that I have a podiatrist for my mouth—I stick my foot in it all the time. If you believe in reincarnation, remember to embrace the teachings and know that you are here to learn and forgive yourself for the things you are not good at. It could very well be one of the reasons you are here right now, in your present life. We are all learning and sometimes it's a slow process.

If your grief is making you feel as though you do not want to forgive yourself or the loved one who has suicided or even if you blame someone else, that's okay. But,

How long do you want to play the blame game?
Is it working for you?
Does it make your life richer?
Are you experiencing joy and happiness with it?

How you respond is up to you. If it's working for you and it is part of your moving on process, okay. From my experience as someone who has personally gone through this and from the experiences shared from thousands of people I've worked with, I've learned this: It takes so much longer to begin to heal when the pointed fingers stay pointed.

It's all right to quit, meaning to quit blaming yourself or others for what cannot be changed.

- *"When does the pain from grief end?"* Unfortunately, there is no finish line. The timetable for resolution is unique to each individual.

- *Why do we grieve?* Because we love and when we have a loved one die, love changes but never ends.

- *Grief has a life of its own.* It shifts and changes, and it can be lighter at times and heavier at times.

- *Grief has its own rhythm.* Like a pendulum, it will move in and out of your life.

- *You are normal.* If you think your grief is making you crazy due to all the emotions and it feels like a roller coaster ride, believe me, you are normal.

- *Own your grief and don't let others dictate your process.*
  We all have our own way of progressing through grief.

Where does grief fit into your everyday life? You will find that it will continue to change. It will take courage to face this challenge, but it is possible to have more good days as time goes on.

Love and grief sound so opposite. It's because of our love that grief exists. It could be one of the biggest challenges in your life, but working through the healing process can be one of the most powerful things you do.

Joy could be one of the most difficult emotions to regain or accomplish, but achieving joy and peace in your heart will allow you to feel, hear, and even see your loved one.

14

Deb's Guideposts for Moving Through Grief

Throughout your lifetime,
you will experience loss.

Below are my nine guideposts in moving through the five stages of grief that Elisabeth Kübler-Ross identified in her book, *On Death and Dying*: **denial, anger, bargaining, depression and acceptance.** The pain that you experienced and may still be feeling is real. My goal is to help you and others through theirs. It's my first guidepost I start with when working with clients.

Guidepost 1. Helping others

If you want to help others through their grief, start with helping yourself ... perhaps even first. Before a commercial airplane takes off, all passengers are reminded in pre-flight instructions that if the overhead oxygen mask releases and drops down ... you are instructed to put YOURS on first, before assisting any others who may need help. You will be better equipped to help others if you have the mental and physical strength to do so.

Many times, clients want to know how to help their children or family members who are also grieving. Since each of them has a different relationship with the individual who has died, it will be different for everyone.

Teaching someone to grieve is by example. As an adult, if you are able to balance the healing and the grief, learn to continue living and celebrating the good things in life as well as mourning the losses, you are teaching others by example. If you are all over the place and seem to have more bad days than good, you do not belong in the place of helping someone else. You aren't ready.

This isn't to say you cannot be concerned or try to be helpful, but allowing another to grieve is his/her right, just like it is yours. If you spend hours and hours worried about someone and you haven't yet taken a look at your grief, then back away and do your work first. Yes, it is natural to worry about others, especially if there has been a suicide. If you are a parent, it's important to remember that you teach by example.

Throughout your lifetime, you will experience loss.

There is no doubt that I've worried about each of my kids and … they have also worried about me. That's what families do to support each other. But, you can't expect children or other family to get better, "over it," or whatever the expectations might be, if you are not willing to walk the talk yourself.

Guidepost 2. What's available?

I find it interesting that many have never dealt with grief. Grief that isn't just about the death of a loved one. Throughout your lifetime, you will experience loss. Think about it. Was there a time that you didn't get picked for a team; you didn't get asked to the prom; there was a divorce within your family (maybe yours); you had to move from a location you loved (either as a child or an adult); you lost a job (either by layoff or termination); or a friendship was suddenly terminated?

Even when we create good things in our lives, there still is a process of grief. Loss also comes with the common stages of life: getting married is the loss of being single; having a child means you will forever be a parent; becoming an empty nester; changing jobs; even selling your home. When we encounter any type of change, we move away from what we knew. How many times do we replace our sadness with something? Having a bad day? Let's have ice cream or go shopping to feel better.

How about when your child's first pet dies? I have done this, and I know others have as well. The goldfish … it dies, and you run to find a look alike, so your child doesn't know his fish Nemo died and has been replaced, right? It may not have been a fish, but as parents seeing your child sad or hurt, you want to fix it.

It is thought that animals don't grieve for long periods of time. Since I'm not a professional on this subject, I only can share with you about Joey. Joey was our Bichon. He grieved terribly after Brad died. We have a two-story home with a walkout basement. After Brad passed, Joey would go down to the patio attached to the walkout basement and sit for hours. Joey just moped around, not eating or playing much. Brad and Joey were connected, and it was clear that Joey missed Brad as well.

I could not deal with Joey being so sad and I worried about his well being. I made a quick decision to get another dog, and the kids were supportive.

I asked Jake and Sophia what they thought. Of course, who doesn't love a new puppy, right? Well, honest and to the point, my amazing kids shared with me, jointly saying, "Mom, we really like this dog and if you want him, we support you. However, we don't help you with Joey so don't expect us to help you with this one."

After checking out the puppy we originally came for, we realized it wasn't going to be a match. Sophia asked, "Do you have any other small puppies?" and that's when we met our newest family member. At three pounds, Jaycee entered our lives and came home with us that night. He has been one of my healing tools and I'm sure Brad helped me in some way. The Sheppard family loves dogs and we all consider them equal.

If you can, take opportunities that come up throughout your life and your children's life to talk about loss and how to manage it. These will be amazing tools with future losses that will eventually come into their lives. No doubt you have experienced loss of some type and how you manage it will help you to bounce back and create new opportunities, not allowing "what is no longer" to control your happiness.

The saying, *things happen for a reason* is not a saying I agree with. I don't think that everything happens for a reason. What you do with your experiences can help you see other ways to manage the life you have. Brad's suicide along with Mat's was horrific for all of us, although we discovered we had a choice: We could let it define our existence and allow it to crumble my children and myself, or we could find ways to maneuver through it. You have those choices as well.

There are so many books, support groups, doctors and even the internet that can provide suggestions and ideas and ways to bring tools to help work through your loss.

The important thing to understand: *You are not alone.* I am here to help. Others are here to help. And you are here now.

Guidepost 3. Giving back is another way to help with the process.

Many, like me, bring awareness to our communities in effort to help others that have traveled the same path. It's one of the thousands of ways to our personal healing and giving back.

There are countless nonprofits that have been created to honor those who have died. If you want to get involved or believe it would also be of benefit to you, join an organization whose mission you believe in, or that has touched you in some way. You will feel supported and realize you are not alone. Try not to feel you have to do it forever or that it's not the right time. It's getting involved in something that can help others and you may be surprised how it can help you as well.

Guidepost 4. Journal your thoughts.

This isn't for everyone, but many individuals like to write what they are experiencing. They keep these thoughts to themselves but may look back later to recall certain moments, and/or note their progression in healing. If you are not seeing changes, it can also give you the awareness that you may want to reach out for additional support.

Guidepost 5. Do something in memory.

Planting a tree, walking for a cause, or creating a photo album are just a few things that you and your family can do together. My family and I support the Suicide Prevention Walk in many places. Chris, Mat's brother, walked in Washington, D.C., and we have walked in Colorado, and have joined others in their walks to support them the best way we possibly can.

Memories are important. Children have favorite times, as do other family members and, of course, you. How you retain, display, and honor memories will be up to you.

Everyday living and working eventually take over. By participating in "memory" interests, you are reminded that your loved one hasn't disappeared; that you are still connected; and that you have not forgotten him or her. When engaging in an important cause, event, or activity, memories will surround you. And, when you participate in them as support of a friend's cause, it shows you haven't forgotten his or her loss either.

Guidepost 6. Take a break from grief!

When loss happens, there are times when you feel like you are taking one step forward, then two (or more!) steps back.

The saying, *How do you eat an elephant? One bite at a time,* fits here. It is important to acknowledge that it's one day at a time and perhaps one day forward in dealing with "things" and then wham—maybe several steps back. Any individual who is making major changes in his or her life can only manage what is in the current moment—not the past or the future. You have no control except the moment you are in.

Give grief a break— you need it and so does your heart.

Taking a break from grief is extremely valuable. Remembering your loved one on every holiday, every event, including anniversaries, can be very taxing. Including your loved ones who are in spirit is a beautiful thing, but it's also okay to just have times where reminders of sadness are not always marked on the calendar.

Many believe that if you are not grieving constantly, that the loved one will feel abandoned, or that you don't miss him or her. Trust me, the loved one has no desire for you to continue to grieve but rather would want to see you happy and having a good life. You would want the same thing if the situation was reversed. *The loved one doesn't desire for you to be in constant pain.* Give grief a break—you need it and so does your heart.

I won't speak for every medium, but at least on my watch I'm quite confident that I haven't had a loved one come through and get upset that my client was not grieving enough for him or her. The loved one may worry about the pain that was caused and that you are still in deep pain or haven't decided to enjoy the things you did before or even new experiences. *Loved ones want you to live a life that brings you joy.*

Often I am asked if it's okay to sell a house; to meet someone new; or to name a new baby with a loved one's name. It's a "yes" to each of these concerns. I get asked questions about what those who have crossed over think about the "stuff" they left behind. I use this example often, "Do you remember your first car?" The client will say, well, yes. I will ask, "Do you know where it is now?" The answer is usually a no.

For most, the first car was your ride to freedom, literally. After a few years you move on to other vehicles. It's very similar to the other side, they are not attached to this physical world you live in and the things that you are attached to. When they cross over, it's not about items. For you, you feel a connection to things you can touch that are reminders of your loved one, "things" that they can't hold and touch any longer. It's your process and your attachment, not for those who have crossed over.

In the beginning of your loss, take small steps and then continue to add longer time periods of allowing yourself to be distracted. Enjoy the world and those that share it with you. They deserve you. No one wants to grieve two losses because one has died and the other doesn't want to heal. Especially if you have children under your care, they deserve to have you present and know it's okay to have happy times, happy sounds, and happy faces.

Guidepost 7. Moving forward!

Previously, I have shared my belief about letting go. I don't feel we have any need or that there is value in letting go. What I have experienced is people feeling as if they can't get better until they let go. That's not what I teach. You are not failing because you are still holding on. You are not keeping your loved one *stuck*. You are not doing something wrong.

My belief is that you try different tools and time passes and you continue to try to heal from your loss, then you just begin to move on with your life, but also hold space in your heart for the one you still love.

Your heart has plenty of room to love many. Since birth, you have loved many people, animals, places, arts, and life experiences, have you not? You are designed to make room for more, not to remove one thing to make room for another. You are not a closet or storage space. It's your heart that creates the unlimited space for love. I have to confess; I wish that worked for my shoe closet.

Your loved one knows you will never forget or replace him or her. Trust me here, it's a message I hear when I meet with clients. A continuous message I carry from those loved ones who have passed is that there is a strong desire to see you love again—and move forward. You may not think it possible, but you always have room for more love. But, it's up to you to add more love to your life.

Guidepost 8. Find your new normal.

Your life has changed. What you desire is to go back to what you had before your loved one died. Friends and clients have shared that they do not like the term: The New Normal. A new normal can mean different things for each individual. Some new normal situations are positive, such as a new baby, a new home or living your dream. But, finding your compass when it comes to the passing of a significant loved one is much more difficult, especially the death of a child at any age. The belief is that your children should be burying you, not the reverse.

Celebrating holidays, the remembrance of anniversaries of the loss, can be a unique challenge when people around you don't understand that you may not have it in you to celebrate. For my children, Father's Day, his birthday, and anniversary of his passing have changed over the years. Christmas was a big holiday for Brad and we will still talk about how he loved to have lots of gifts under the tree for everyone.

I've heard it is the same for parents who have had children die, that Mother's Day and Father's Day are very difficult to acknowledge even when they have other children.

If you are supporting someone who has had a loss, ask them what they would like to do instead of you assuming what they need. If you are the person that is grieving, let others know what you would like. It doesn't have to be the same thing every year because you are just learning about this thing called grief.

Allow your "new normal" to change through time just like you will. Make it about you and what is comfortable for your healing process. The first Christmas we wanted to do something very different because he had only been gone less than two months. We ended up in Vegas which was very different. Not sure that was the best destination for two young people and myself, but we did it, and the kids had a blast.

We did get a little push back from others about our choice, but that was the point. It was our choice how we wanted to experience this first Christmas without their father. Try many things to find your new normal, the point here that it's new. And it's yours for the making.

Guidepost 9. Listen to your heart.

Your heart, even when in great pain, can give you direction. Take the time to be in the moment and listen to your soul. You may need to be alone to figure out what you need. If you have someone who can process with you, it can be very helpful.

Few want to hear those words: *It will take time.* Yes, it takes time. It takes nine months to bring a baby into this world and rushing the arrival of a baby is not a good thing. And rushing what you are feeling and experiencing is not a good thing. If you can give yourself permission to process through your bereavement, and to heal, your heart will speak to you with a gentle voice. Just listen.

Guideposts are merely that—guides. They are not set in stone, but are ideas and supports. The nine I've listed above are not in a "must do" sequence. What I do know is that you will touch on many, or even all, during this time.

15

Taking Care of Your Mind, Body, and Spirit

*The purpose of meditation is to be present—
in the moment, in the now.*

Grief looks different for everyone and the healing can be as unique as each individual. For those trying new techniques or leaning into what they used to do in their daily life can be helpful in the process.

If you never have experienced any spiritual modality, such as meditation, then it may be a little challenging, but don't give up on it. It is different for everyone. And it can take some time to feel comfortable using this new tool.

Meditation doesn't have to look like the monks who live in a temple where they have very few distractions in their daily lives. While sitting in the lotus position, fingers in position resting on your knees while doing mantras is a wonderful technique for some. However, for most, this can just be uncomfortable and frustrating. A lotus position could be equivalent to a foreign language.

Even during your regular day, you can meditate while doing the things that are common for you. When I'm blow drying my hair, I can become present and begin transition into a meditation. This doesn't mean my mind is 100 percent clear of thoughts. I'm actually processing whatever comes into my head. I allow it to flow in and out with little rationalizing. There is no arguing with myself and trying to figure out what I'm hearing.

The purpose of meditation is to be present—in the moment, in the now. Most of you have so many lists of things to do every day, it's no wonder that you become overwhelmed and are unable to quiet your mind. Play some soothing music, light a candle, wear comfortable clothing and have the room at a good temperature for you. Adult coloring books were introduced several years ago and have become bestsellers in book selling. Get a few and let your creativity flow and your mind wander. Being comfortable; not dealing with an environment that is too hot or too cold; listening to your favorite music; even surrounding yourself with favorite aromas all create an ideal environment to "just let go" ... you are not distracted so you can color, journal, and learn to become present. These are some things I've always recommended.

In the beginning, don't set an agenda. As your new routine becomes more normal, then—and only then—introduce an intention to what you are doing. If you desire to connect with your loved one, this is a way to begin. Keep a notepad or write on the back of the picture you are coloring on as you feel, hear, or see things.

It will feel as if you are making it up, but please trust the process. Try not to control an outcome. This is how it works. And if it is something new that you are experiencing, it can feel awkward, even unbelievable. I also recommend that you try connecting with others you know who have passed, perhaps not the significant loved one you are really wanting to connect with.

What comes forth may surprise you. They may show you images in your mind; you could hear things; feel and even smell aromas that will let you know they are present. This can begin your way of staying connected to your loved one.

There is no wrong way to meditate. If you enjoy the outdoors, then connect with Mother Earth. No matter where you live or work, go outside and feel the sun. Enjoy looking at nature. It not only can bring up your spirits but can support your wish of becoming centered, so you can heal and if desired, connect with your loved one/s.

Healing from the loss of a loved one takes energy to help the mind, body, and spirit.

Playing music, cooking, sinking into a hot Epsom salt bath, taking a hot shower, swimming, even vacuuming are all possible ways to relax and center.

You can take classes for meditation or buy an instructional DVD, and find helpful background music online. You may feel a little guilt adding "time for you" into your routine if you are very busy. When you are trying to quiet your mind and your body, let guilt step aside. And surprisingly, you will discover that you gain more energy and have more clarity, so things can get done more efficiently.

Healing from the loss of a loved one, takes energy to help the mind, body, and spirit.

Taking care of your entire being is vital for your healing. Caring for all parts of you may be difficult for many reasons. Others may need you, or think they do. There could be guilt you are carrying because of his or her death. If you can show your process to others, they will give themselves permission to take care of their needs as well. Perhaps, you can do these things together so you can all feel supported.

Doctors and many healing facilities provide B-12 injections which could help your body. Drinking a lot of water with added electrolytes, eating organic foods, and doing some form of exercise will help in so many ways. If you are not one that loves to exercise or sweat at a gym, try walking a few blocks in the neighborhood, putting small weights on your ankles and wrists and taking the stairs whenever possible. Stretching and taking deep breaths throughout the day will provide more energy and clarity for your body and mind to heal.

Grief is located in our hearts. If we can support both our body and soul, it will help our heart. Our minds can then begin to process. The result: We start to bring peace into our minds.

There is no straight path to alleviating and eliminating grief. It will take many twist and turns. Be patient with yourself and others around you. There is no magic potion to protect you from this journey that is called grief.

16

Dealing with Unwanted Advice and Comments

Have boundaries and set them
for others if they don't have them.

Have you ever been in a situation where others express opinions about something without knowing what really happened; or having any understanding of the circumstances; or even any knowledge about the "situation"? One of the difficulties of grieving a loss from a suicide is the judgment that seems to coattail on the pain of those left behind.

Although it's not appropriate for them to share, many times people who share their opinions or tell you what you "should" be doing are trying to make themselves feel better in the situation of a loss.

It's not uncommon for family and spouses to be private when there is a suicide. Many may not share that their loved one suicided because of how others may react. A sense of shame may be felt. If their religion has taught them to believe that there is punishment for those who take their own life, this may be a factor. When an individual has had a loss from suicide, the worse thing people can say is anything relating to a reprimand or penalty of some sorts. When my mother-in-law died from heart failure, a woman and her daughter approached me at her service, sharing their condolences. The mother said, "The only lame thing I can say is, I'm sorry."

I hugged her and said, "That's all anyone needs to ever say." It's no different with suicide. For some reason, there are always going to be those people who are somehow compelled to share when they haven't been invited, believing they have words of wisdom. The question is, for whom?

A simple and heartfelt "I'm sorry" goes a long way.

Often, these "words of wisdom" are "words of ignorance" coming out of the mouths of individuals who are not aware of what others are going through. What is needed is sympathy and comfort.

If you believe that someone will go to hell if he or she passed by suicide, keep it to yourself. If you feel you want to provide advice, my advice is don't! However, if you have experienced it or have been trained to understand grief, especially around suicide, then ask the person grieving if you can share. If the person is in a place to hear your advice and asks you to, then please do. But, the best thing I can suggest to you is this: Ask if the person wants to share with you ... then talk about that person's loved one. Can you also listen without input and without judgment? That is what the person needs—a compassionate heart, without the judgment.

If someone dies from a heart attack, an accident, or cancer, people give their condolences. When it comes to suicide, it's an entirely unique situation. There's hesitation, even reluctance, to reach out.

A simple and heartfelt "I'm sorry" goes a long way. You might ask a person to share something—a pleasant memory—about the loved one. This will help by providing an opportunity to heal instead of making the person feel more guilt and regret.

Few of us want to be judged; rather we want to be accepted and feel safe. But, for some reason, there are those that feel very comfortable with giving an opinion about something on which they know nothing.

If you are on the receiving end and you have experienced this, there are things you can say to manage the situation. If someone wants to give you advice that you don't want to hear, and the person begins without asking, say something like:

"Thanks for sharing," and leave it alone with no further response.

"I am not really in a place to receive advice right now, but I appreciate your thinking of me. Perhaps you can share at another time."

Or, "I have heard so much advice, I'm on overload. Do email it to me. When it's a better time for me, I will look at it." Then you can just delete it and tell them thanks for sharing.

You can even reach over and touch person's arm to show your appreciation, and say, "It's not a good time for me to talk."

There will be times when you are left stunned and speechless with what someone says. When you come to your senses, you'll wish that you had kicked that person in the shins; delivered a verbal zinger or two; or even flipped him or her off. Yes, I know that may seem a bit crude, but you are dealing with you and your feelings. There certainly have been times in your life when you have had "head responses" with others but never actually said out loud what you thought. If you perceive that you are being emotionally abused by people's comments, then very likely you are. Your gut will know.

Here's what is okay: You can let people know that they have crossed your boundaries; that their comments are inappropriate. Never forget: You have every right to do so.

Being in the public, I'm still asked about my husband. What happened? Why couldn't I have seen it coming? Why didn't Jake want to know about how his father passed? Do I hear from Brad now? I certainly didn't want to share. There would be times I would have hundreds of guests at a class and someone wanted to have a deep conversation or just ask these questions. These were questions a person was curious about with not really thinking how I might feel.

You have permission to do what you need for your grief.

Interestingly, I believe there was a combination of curiosity and an attempt to be supportive, but I wasn't asking for the person's support. Normally, I would just say, "I'm not in a place to share with you right now. I'm here to work with others." I have 200 guests waiting for me to speak and someone wants to discuss the loss of my husband! Seriously, this doesn't make sense.

It's okay not to share if you don't want. You do not owe another person an explanation. If the person is offended, well, so are you. It's not your problem, it's his or hers and you have no obligation to explain or help that person feel better. You have permission to do what you need for your grief.

When advice is given, or comments made, you can pivot the conversation. You can take this time to educate someone about suicide. Reveal information that it's an illness and that so many are dying from depression and perhaps he or she would like to donate or become involved in Suicide Awareness. Refer that person to the American Foundation for Suicide Prevention for information, or any other organization that you may be involved in or want to support.

What you do and say is up to you. You are not being rude. You have every right to respond the way you feel. I find that at times I can share, and other times I'm just not in a place to talk about it.

Death of any sort—but especially suicide—can be a sensitive topic when talking to young people. If it's your kids, you decide how to manage it, not someone else. They are your children; you know them best. When it comes to others, talk to the surviving parent or the guardians about how to approach the subject if you are in a position to be interacting with the children. As I share in this book, the loved one died by *mind cancer,* not brain cancer. They did not "commit suicide" they "died by suicide." Their mind was ill, and they passed because of it.

If you are going to post on social media, be careful. The invisible shield that social media allows creates the opportunity for people to post comments, pictures, videos—you name it— that can be hurtful. While healing from your loss, there is no need for people's opin-

Why am I trying so hard to get approval when they weren't in the situation?

ions that don't support you and your family. This is about taking care of you and those that are grieving the loss.

After Brad died, I received a lot of opinions from others or heard things later that were hurtful, because they didn't know the circumstances or what I was juggling. Things like, "Why did she have his service so quickly after he died?" "Why did she spend the first Christmas the year after he passed that way?" "Why is she handling her kids the way she is?" And my personal favorite: "She isn't grieving the right way." Really—just what is the right way?

All inappropriate questions and comments. The reality is that when there is a death in a home—whether it's from an accident, illness, natural cause or a suicide—the outside world does not know what is going on within the inside world of those connected to the deceased. When you are dealing with a death of any type, why do others think they know what is right or the right way for you? They don't. These types of comments only create more guilt for those dealing with the loss. And they can actually set them back in processing processing their grief.

At first, I tried to explain my reasoning, so I did want approval and acceptance. Then, I began to question myself. Why was I trying so hard to get approval when they weren't in the situation? They hadn't been living in my nightmare where I had and watched the man I loved fade away in front of my eyes. I learned I didn't need to explain my reasons for my choices. If they were wrong, I dealt with them. I chose to accept my decisions and move forward.

Most of the time, people have good intentions. At times of stress, many do not think before they open their mouths. With some of the comments that were made directly to me, I know I would have a look of *What the f***!* But then realized that the "What the f***!" look I had directed at the person was never understood—the person didn't get *my look, my nonverbal* response.

When Brad first passed, people would want to come to my house or call me asking for details. They wanted to know everything! And many wouldn't stop when I tried to ignore them or change the subject. Surprisingly, some wanted to know details— acting as if they had the inside story; wanting to hear all the dirt and nitty-gritty. They were like rubber-neckers ... people who drive past an automobile accident and slow down to see the terrible situation.

Because I had a large community, it seemed some individuals wanted to know the inside scoop so they could tell others, so it would appear that they knew more than everyone else. Ugh! I was sometimes so overwhelmed, I would share my feelings and thoughts and then they would leave quickly to tell others. I have since learned to not be so open to "casual" friends and acquaintances; to share little unless it's someone I feel has my back. I would suggest you do the same.

The bottom line: You need to have boundaries and set them for others if they don't have them.

What Not to Say to Someone Grieving

'm going to be blunt about this topic. This is a page you should copy and keep. And please, don't be shy about giving it to others. Ask those who are grieving if they have been told or asked any of the following.

What NOT to Say or Ask

1. He/she is in a better place.
2. Everything happens for a reason.
3. God wanted him/her with him.
4. I lost my dog (or whomever or whatever) to cancer last year.
5. I understand how you feel.
6. It's time to move on.
7. It's time to get over it.
8. I'll pray for you.
9. Don't compare your losses to theirs.
10. It will get better.
11. It was meant to be.
12. I can imagine what you are going through.
13. Can I have some of his/her things?

---

14. When are you going to get out there again?
15. Eventually, everyone dies.
16. He/she must have done something to deserve this.
17. Well, he/she will pay the price when meeting God.
18. You can pay for more prayers to make sure your loved one goes to a good place.
19. God must have a plan for you.
20. What was he/she thinking?
21. Don't you feel guilty?
22. Did he/she believe in God?
23. What happened?
24. Is there anything you could have done to prevent this from happening?

Bottom line, don't give advice, your opinion, or compare your loss with someone else's. Don't ask questions that add to the hurt and confusion that those who are left are experiencing. Ask if the person would like to hear your advice or suggestions. But if the person doesn't appear to be seriously interested, then back off. Keep whatever you were thinking or going to say to yourself. Perhaps, later the person will approach you and ask for your ideas. In the meantime, just be a good listener. Ask questions and don't respond except to say, "I'm so sorry."

What to say? Choose:
I'm so sorry for your loss. How can I be of support to you?

That's it!

Questions that you possibly could ask if a person is open to sharing include:

1. What did you love about him/her?
2. What things will you miss most?
3. What do you need help with?
4. What is a fond memory of him/her that pops into your head?

Let the person know that he or she can reach out to you any time and just talk. It could be very comforting to a grieving person to hear you say that. Let the person know that you will reach out in days ahead, but he/she does not have to respond. It is his/her choice.

After Brad passed, I received an invitation from a neighbor who was also my husband's previous boss' wife. She invited me to some sort of Tupperware, makeup or whatever home party. It had only been a few weeks and there was no way I was in a position to attend. I didn't RSVP. I'm not sure if they attended his memorial service to pay their respects. There were over 500 in attendance and the day quickly became a blur.

A month had passed and I saw my neighbor at the grocery store. She said hello, and I asked if she heard about Brad. She replied yes, and added, "You didn't attend my party. I thought it would help you to be at the gathering." She didn't say, "I'm so sorry, what can I do, or how were my kids?" She did not reach out in a way that might have been helpful to me with two kids who might need something. Her daughter had babysat my kids over the years. Nothing about sharing a meal, bringing a meal, or just a "How are you doing? Is there something I can help you with?" Nope, there was no extension of kindness in the conversation.

I left feeling as if his death was invisible and that this person didn't care about anything except keeping up with the neighborhood. Did she expect me to act as if nothing had happened … to fit back in? I was dumbfounded.

I learned to realize that there are many people who are actually ignorant about handling such a tragedy. They have no reality other than their own immediate surroundings and circumstances.

It's very heartbreaking to me that some people believe if they don't acknowledge death that it won't affect them. Eventually, it will happen to all of us. We don't get out of losing our loved ones and most don't know how to help someone else until it happens to them. Someday, my neighbor could be in my same shoes ...

Do you know someone who is happy to give parenting advice but who has never had a child? And there are those who have never walked on a particular path, but are still wanting to give non-solicited advice. I find this interesting.

The same holds true when others offer their opinions about loss. If they haven't experienced it, it's best if they just keep their ideas, thoughts, and questions to themselves. But support is appreciated.

Less is more in this situation!

18

My Work
as a Medium

*As a Medium, I have a natural ability
to feel, see, and hear your loved one much easier.*

Seeking a medium can be controversial. Many people may have religious conflicts or disbelief that one can actually connect with your departed. Mediums have become more mainstream since TV shows, books, radio, and large public events have featured mediums. People are looking for answers and closure, so the idea of seeking a medium has become acceptable to many who didn't know about them before, were skeptical, or previously rejected the idea.

If you are considering seeking the connection of a medium and it's your first time, do your research. Not all who claim to be one *are* authentic and understanding the terminology is very important. The title "Psychic" doesn't always mean they are a "Medium." Actually, there is a big difference. A medium has an ability to channel those who have crossed over, along with the ability to interpret messages from your loved ones through vision, smell, sound, touch, and feel. All mediums are psychic but all psychics are not mediums.

Psychics can channel as well, but most do not have the same level of ability as a medium does. It doesn't mean that they are not great psychics, it's just a difference in what they can do. A psychic will typically help you find clarity in your everyday life as opposed to the array of abilities that a medium will have.

I have been blessed by many in the medical community—supporting and referring and encouraging their clients to work with me as a medium. Therapists, psychologists, and other healers have all seen positive results when I work to help a client through grief. It's wonderful that we can work together to assist someone in his or her healing. My work over the years has shown me that it can take multiple modalities to help people with their grief.

A medium isn't a grief counselor unless he or she has been trained through professional programs. However, I as a medium will offer advice since I am helping so many through their healing process.

For me, messages come from things I understand in my life. I have built a language with the other side, so I can interpret the messages they are trying to communicate. Remember, those who have crossed over do not have bodies or vocal cords. What I *see* and *hear* come from my memory and my experiences. I will be shown images in my mind—even images from movies as an example with one client. I will see a house and take a piece of paper and draw it, including the exterior detail.

In this instance, what I was being shown was the house from the movie, *A Christmas Story*. When I revealed it to the person I was working with, he and his siblings validated that it was just like their grandmother's home. They didn't know I saw the picture from the movie, but that's how I communicated with their loved one. I "see things" that make sense to me and then do my very best to translate the details to my clients.

Sometimes information coming through won't be validated immediately during a session. Sometimes clients receiving information could not recall the information during their session, but later it became very clear. Those are aha signs that I believe are amazing. The only way I would know these things is if their loved one told me.

When a loss such as when a suicide has occurred, those left behind can be challenged in their belief system. If they have been taught that suicide means the soul is stuck and is being punished or in hell, it can be overwhelming and perhaps feel as if their loved one is still suffering. For the thousands of sessions I've held, I have been honored to connect with loved ones and have never felt the individual that died was in any pain.

Everything is energy, and you can't create it or destroy it.

Other family members, friends, and beloved pets come through together, sharing that they are all united and at peace, and without pain.

When I've been asked about how they are doing, I always say, "There's no dieting or taxes, so how bad can it be?" My intention in using humor is to show that they are truly okay now and they are not suffering as they were here when physically with us. Their bodies no longer exist, we are connecting with their souls. And their souls are intact.

Many clients will ask why they can't hear or feel their loved ones? There are multiple reasons, but know that you can learn to hear from them and see the signs they are trying to give you. They want to connect with you and most likely they have been trying.

As a Medium, I have a natural ability to feel, see, and hear your loved one much easier. I am not connected to the grief and all the emotions that come with your loss.

As a Medium, even I can struggle sometimes with feeling my loved ones because I am dealing with the same concerns.

By healing and shifting your energy, you can begin to connect yourself. It is electricity, sound, radio waves and the undiscovered frequency that energy science is trying to find. This means that the vibrational frequency in which we vibrate will attract that vibration to us and vice versa. What are you attracting with your thought and feeling vibrations?

The Universe is energy. You can't create it or destroy it. This means that everything contains energy—everything. Energy has a frequency creating connections that you are aware of … and unaware of. It does this with vibrations. Imagine a radio broadcast. When you are in different locations, you can pick up different stations, and the ones you pick up may be at different strengths. If you travel to an area where the frequency can no longer be heard, it means that the frequency vibration has changed.

Have you ever encountered individuals and "felt something?" It could be an attraction. You want to know more about them and be around them. Or, have you had a sense that you should distance yourself as if you can't get away fast enough? Your energy frequencies are talking to you.

The Signs of Presence

When you have a loss of a loved one, your human process of grief has many layers: denial, anger, shock or disbelief, bargaining, guilt, depression, acceptance, and hope. These are never in the same order, which is why people are always at different stages for the same loss. You may not embrace the full healing process, and only deal with a few of the stages. If you do decide not to take these steps or at least most of them, it can be more challenging to hear from your loved ones.

There is no right or wrong way for anyone, but this explains why there could be a challenge for someone who wants to hear from his or her family. Many times, just having one session with a medium will let you begin healing by knowing that your loved ones are at peace and they see what is still going on in your life. This can allow you to begin looking for the signs and trusting they are really with you.

Signs from your loved ones can be very simple things. For me, I've found pennies in my shower, and on the floor where I walked past a dozen times in one day. One morning, I woke up and my slipper had a handful of pennies in it. Brad always had coins around and even a small suit case of his grandfather's filled with old pennies. Ten years have passed and I still see pennies in the oddest places.

You cannot demand that your loved one show up and give you signs for you to believe.

What I know is that your loved ones want to make their presence known to you. It's just being able to be open to it and then allowing them to show up. To be honest, when I teach students to understand their abilities as a medium, I begin by sharing that it feels as if you are making it up. This is why it can be difficult to trust what occurs. That's how it really feels, so keep an open mind and just notice the things around you.

You cannot demand that one or several show up and expose signs for you to believe. If you couldn't make him or her do what you wanted when alive, do you think you have that kind of power when crossing over happens? It's not unusual for a client to have a session and during the hour, multiple validations come through woven with details that only the client and loved one know. If there had been a request to validate a specific thing during the session and it wasn't responded to, disbelief surfaces. It always saddens me because it doesn't always work the way the client desires. If it's something I can't connect to, then I may not be able to translate the request back.

Sometimes my client isn't a loved one. It could be law enforcement. Throughout the years, cold cases and missing person cases come to me. It takes my ability to a different level and it's work that I've always done pro-bono for the police department and families involved. Sometimes it's initiated by a detective; other times a family member will contact me. In that case, I refer them back to the detective assigned to the case in order to grant me permission to work with him/her. It is very interesting work to say the least.

I share messages that specifically apply to your loved ones. This happens often, and I love it when I receive a call or email validating the message. It's about trusting what I receive even if the client wants to hear other information. Your loved one does see what is occurring in your life right now and will share those things with me to tell you. My clients reveal that it gives one a sense of peace knowing they are still around.

My favorite messages to share are the odd ones, because they are unique to you. Generic information can come through all the time, but a good medium will provide specific information that is directly for you from your loved one. It may not be a nickname or a unique vacation spot or favorite book, but it will be unique. And you will recognize it.

Creating a Successful Medium Experience

No medium is more gifted or special than anyone else on this planet. One of our goals is to provide a message of peace to you, so your healing can continue. Can it get blocked or diverted?

Yes. When a client tries to control the session the way he/she wants or feels it should go, it normally isn't successful for either the client or myself as the medium. It is as if the hose gets kinked and it may prevent your loved one on the other side from successfully communicating. It's similar to going to a restaurant and heading to the kitchen to tell the chef how to cook. You need to be open to suggestions from the menu, and look forward to what's presented on your plate. You are there to satisfy your hunger and enjoy the taste. Aren't you?

As with any profession: Let the experts do their job, and you will have a successful appointment. While we try to educate our clients weeks before their session, we have many who will still try to be in the driver's seat. It's always interesting, but I think it's all about trusting the process of allowing others to help.

How many times should someone see a medium and how often? It's a common question. The answer is: It will depend on the situation. If it is the process of normal grief that is being experienced, I believe a therapist or licensed professional would be the appropriate place to start. And, I don't encourage someone to seek a medium on a regular basis to connect with the same loved one.

Seeing a medium once is good. And if you would like future sessions, no matter where you are in your healing process, I encourage that you work on healing and learning to connect on your own. Unless the medium you are working with is a licensed therapist, it would be his/her call and ethics of that medium. Some of my clients make appointments on a birthday or anniversary of their loved one, which I find to be just fine. Normally, after a few of these, they move on with their grief and healing.

When a client chooses to work with me, I employ a specific code of ethics; one I feel is extremely important. In my practice,

I believe it's an honor to provide a message to a client. And before I do, I ask permission. I do not just openly give messages until the client says he/she is ready to receive it.

In any business when an individual is good at something, the ego can tag along. I believe we need our ego to live our lives. It has great value, but as long as our life is not ego driven, with a belief that it, meaning you, is superior to another.

My belief is that every individual brings something very special to this planet, and together, we make most things work. It is a collective blessing. When someone describes or calls what I do *a gift*, I think otherwise. What I have is *an ability*. We all have abilities that we can decide to share with the world or not. I share mine. Yes, working with you and with your loved one is a collective blessing. And I thank you for the privilege of bringing your loved ones' messages into my world and sharing them with you.

19

Afterword ...
and Thriving

*My journey in this life has never been
on a straight and narrow path.*

wanted to find love again—a partner who wasn't my project.
I didn't want to take care of someone, but someone where we
could take care of each other. After lots and lots of dating, I did
find true love. Several years ago, I had written a letter as if I was
writing to my love. It talked about what I see in that person and
how we are being together and our children cared about each
other—a blended family that loved and supported one another.
After meeting my life partner, I found that letter. It was as if I
had been writing about her.

This was a total surprise to me. I never imagined that I
would have a female partner. I have lost many friends and family
over the years because of choices I've made and the work I do.
But, I'm the happiest I have ever been and that's what everyone
should want for me and for anyone they love.

Dana is an amazing and talented professional in so many ways.
She and Sophia have taken on my practice and have completely

changed how I now work. My support system is incredible and I'm continuing to heal in multiple ways. Her son Thomas is the same age as Sophia. The three kids have become very close and love having their mothers happy. We call each other *Om*—for original mother and other mother.

My journey in this life has never been on a straight and narrow path. I share that I have a mosaic path because I've done many unique things that I never would have imagined as a teenager that I would do.

We can only respond to what happens in our lives, we cannot control others or an outcome that we think is best.

I'm grateful that I can be a messenger from loved ones to the living. And I am grateful that I am able to have true love once again. I am honored that I am a mother and have been able to support my children through a horrific time in their lives and to see how amazing they have grown up.

None of our journeys are over yet. We have many more years ahead of us. But, what I have learned is we can only respond to what happens in our lives, we cannot control others or an outcome that we think is best.

I've learned not to assume or judge others for their life choices and to accept my limitations. It's not with guilt, but with knowing I have the courage to overcome many of life's challenges. And I celebrate being thankful for what I have and embrace being more in the moment versus contemplating what's ahead or what has happened in the past.

Humor to me is always the best tool in anyone's tool box. My mother has a great sense of humor, which is a blessing she gave me. Don't be afraid of bringing laughter to your life, especially when you are healing.

Life takes all of us on different paths and most of these paths are unexpected. What you do with these experiences is up to you. If you will look deep into your heart and trust yourself, and not look for approval or acceptance of those around you, then life can certainly take a turn to true healing.

It's up to you to decide how you want to live. Those that we love who have suicided may have felt that they weren't good enough and that the judgment from others was so difficult to manage that they didn't want to live any longer.

What if we as a society accepted those that are not the same? Would the number of suicides, drugs addicts, and alcoholics decrease? If we as a society changed our beliefs about mental illness, become more accepting of others, there is no doubt in my heart and soul that our world would change for the better.

Are you ready to thrive? What are you going to do differently to make that happen?

Deb Sheppard
Medium. Psychic. Author. Speaker.

forever connected
bringing life full circle

Deb Sheppard, internationally recognized medium, psychic, author, and speaker, has connected thousands of clients to their loved ones in spirit, helping bring life full circle. Death is a part of every life, and Deb believes those who have crossed over remain connected to us––although they are on the other side, they are forever by our side.

What makes Deb Sheppard different? She can use all of her senses to access information from the other side. Using her acute skills of Clairvoyance, Clairaudience, Clairsentience, Clairscent, Clairgustance, Clairtangency, Clairempathy, and Channeling, she can see, feel, hear, smell, taste, touch and channel as she interprets messages. Deb believes we are all energy and she can connect with any energy. She also connects with animals and those still living on the earthly plane.

Deb's incredible ability places her in the top 3% most accurate in her profession. She has been tested and is recommended by James Van Praagh and is recommended by *Best Psychic Directory* as a top-rated Medium.

Known also as an "empath," Deb connects to the unseen realms through feelings in her body and her emotions. As a medium, she acts as a liaison, relaying comforting messages between the physical and spiritual worlds, communicating with people and animals who have crossed over. Deb's sense of humor, light-heartedness, and compassion create a safe and fun environment for all who attend her readings and events.

Since 2001, her detailed readings have amazed and astounded many around the world. Her belief is to help empower all the people that she works with so they can break free of the fears that hold them back from being their true selves. She has guided and taught thousands of students her philosophy on the afterlife, how we can open communication with the spirit world and move forward in a much more enlightened, passionate, and inspired way.

Her journey into mediumship began unexpectedly, when she and her husband had relocated to Colorado and were facing financial difficulty. Her family was on the verge of losing everything. She decided to look for answers outside of her life experiences––and the answers came: Deb began to feel spirits who had crossed over and, after much reading and exploring, soon realized she was a medium. Her skill would become a comfort to millions of listeners, viewers, and followers.

Deb believes that you can live multiple lifetimes in one life and that no matter where you are on your journey, you can change your life once you open yourself to receiving. Whether you call it intuition, ability, God, Spirit, Divine, Energy, Universe, or a higher power of any kind, Deb believes you can connect if YOU are open to the answers.

Deb has a mission to prevent suicide

One of her most passionate missions is to help prevent suicide and aide suicide awareness through numerous efforts and organizations. Deb's life has been touched multiple times by suicide, and she intends to help change the stigma surrounding this in her work going forward. In fact, the *Grieving to Believing* book expresses her depth of understanding of the subject.

Many of Deb's clients are drawn to her because they, too, have been deeply affected by suicide. Much of her work focuses on helping people cope with grief and guilt when a loved one has died by suicide or helping them understand the mental illness that may have caused it. She also helps those contemplating such an act to find the hope, inner empowerment and purpose to live, and to live fully.

Deb has been the featured speaker on the topic of suicide for multiple organizations and at numerous events, such as the Young Professionals Organization, Survivors of Suicide, Women in Business with Mrs. Sandy Dahl (widow of Captain Jason Dahl, the pilot of United Airlines flight 93 on 9/11), and at Cherokee Castle & Ranch in Sedalia, Colorado. Annually, Deb is involved with the American Foundation for Suicide Prevention, including its "Out of Darkness Walk" along with emceeing The Chelsea Hutchison Foundation Gala for epilepsy and SUDEP awareness.

Deb's additional highlights
as a speaker and celebrity

The media enjoys the richness and clarity Deb brings to viewers and listeners on any broadcast which features her. She has been featured on Denver-based *KOSI 101.1* for 15 years, participating in both late night and morning show segments.

As a frequent guest on a variety of TV and radio shows, repeat appearances have been on *KUSA-TV* Channel 9 in Denver, including "Colorado & Company," *Fox 31* Denver, and KRQE in Albuquerque, New Mexico, and appearing on *Studio 59* with NFL superstar Von Miller.

She has been featured on several iHeart Radio stations including *95.7 The Party, JJ & Deanna Show,* and *Deb Nabb's The Mutt Master* show, where she communicates with animals and pet parents that have challenges. For six years, she worked with Jones Radio Networks, her readings being syndicated on 150 national stations.

Several publications have also highlighted Deb, her philosophies and spiritual understandings: *The Healing Path Magazine*, which also featured John Holland; *Orbs A Personal Journey* by Donna Didomenico; *Good to Go: A Guide to Preparing for End of Life* by Jo Myers; and *My Loved One Shines On, a Gift from Beyond* by Disa Van Orman. The *Albuquerque Journal* and *Westword* in Denver have featured articles about Deb and the impact she has made on so many.

As a popular keynote presenter for a variety of organizations and companies, including the Young Professional Organization, Deb mesmerizes her audiences. For more than 20 years, she has hosted workshops, classes and events with small and large groups. These self-improvement workshops focus on helping clients overcome life's challenges in order to create the most fulfilling lives possible.

Deb Sheppard is recognized as one of the top in her profession. She is eager through *Grieving to Believing* and "Forever Connected" Tour—to share her abilities internationally and help others on a global scale.

To contact her, check her availability or follow her blog, visit her website:

www.DebSheppard.com
Dana@DebSheppard.com | 720-315-5235

How to Work with Deb Sheppard

As one of the most recognized physic mediums, Deb Sheppard has made the difference in millions of individuals lives. Her events are sold-out weeks before they occur.

Dedicated to the prevention of suicide, Deb is regularly involved with the American Foundation for Suicide Prevention, including its "Out of Darkness Walk" event each year.

The media features her on television and radio shows. As a featured speaker for organizations and private groups, she brings a unique ability to draw in an audience with her wisdom and humor while engaging them with thought provoking and life enhancing topics.

Visit her website and subscribe to her blog at:

www.DebSheppard.com

Connect with her on:

 DebSheppardPychicMedium

 Medium Deb Sheppard @DebSheppard1

For the Media Requests and to Book All Events and Speaking Engagements, contact: Dana Nieto at *Dana@DebSheppard.com* 720-315-5235

For a Private Session with Deb Sheppard, contact
Info@DebSheppard.com | 720-315-5235

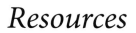

Resources

How to Choose a Good Medium

If you are interested in seeking out a medium, here are a few things that I would recommend you ask, get answered, and understand.

1. Should you see a medium?

If you are worried that you will be judged or the response may be very critical, then ask as if you are just curious. Such as, have you ever watched *Medium* on TV? If they say yes, reply by asking, what do you think about mediums? Depending on the response, you can follow up by asking if the person has ever been to one or is aware of a local medium. If asked why, reply that you have been interested in understanding things and searching for answers since your recent loss. Play it low key and remember, you may hear every type of response, and you will be the only one that can decide if seeking a medium is right for you.

2. Is this something you desire to do on your own or with someone who can attend with you?

During a session with me, you can have multiple people in attendance, but expect that each will be charged. And information will come through for everyone present. Your loved ones will come through regardless of who paid, so having multiple people in the session is similar to a private session. You just share the time together. If you are in the room, always someone everyone loves comes through.

3. Do you feel that seeking a medium is against your religious beliefs?

Most mediums respect the differences in beliefs that others hold. We have no intention of changing your beliefs or feel as if we need you to believe us. It's truly about being the messenger and allowing you to decide what you leave with from the experience.

Mediums realize that they are always being judged for their abilities, which comes with the territory. If we take it too personally and try to prove ourselves, we will get in the way of channeling your loved ones.

4. Are you skeptical about seeing a medium?

Be skeptic, but be open. Even I am a skeptic when it comes to psychics and mediums. Just as in any business, there are great ones—teachers, doctors, police officers, artists, chefs, writers, computer programmers—and others you wouldn't cross the street to meet.

Occasionally I will visit psychics/mediums myself. I do this when I travel for a couple of reasons. One, to see if I can hear things that I need to see about myself and to remind me what it feels like to be the client, to sit in the chair across from the reader.

It should never be scary or contain information that doesn't make you feel good. A session is to bring about a level of peace and perhaps tools to help you along your journey.

5. Are you open?

This doesn't mean you should believe everything the medium shares with you. If most of the session feels on the mark, then that's a good session. If there are pieces of it that didn't resonate with you or doesn't make sense at the time, just file it away for later. As I mentioned before, sometimes you will be able to validate the messages you receive later on, so be open. It's not a science, at least not for now.

Remember, when you get advice from a professional, many times there is a latitude of gray area, such as when taking your car to a repair shop, hiring a plumber or even seeking guidance from your physician. Even with lab tests, computers, and high technology, most professionals are doing their best to provide you with insight from their knowledge and experiences plus the results they have in front of them. It's the same scenario with mediums and psychics. Our intention is to provide the best information that we can understand at the moment the messages are given.

Experienced mediums will have had years to learn and fine tune their craft, such as any experienced professional you seek will have more knowledge and experiences to drawn upon. As we know, no human-being is perfect, and this can help you be open to your session as well as take away the messages that provide a little more for your healing process.

6. How many times should you seek a medium?

This answer to this question is up to you. However, I do not encourage clients to return often, unless they have had more losses, or they have so many who have crossed that all of them didn't show in the first session. With that said, going to a therapist, a grief group, or seeking support in other ways is much more vital then seeking a medium over and over again. Mediums are normally not licensed therapists and, in my opinion, there should be ethics and boundaries regarding seeing a client over and over without encouraging their client to seek other resources.

7. What do you need to do to prepare for a session?

Whether you are doing a private session or attending a group reading, in my opinion it is vital for everyone to do a little preparation. When scheduling an appointment with me, my team will ask the client to go to my website and read the section on "How to Prepare for a Medium Session." Even during a large group reading, I will also provide a little insight about the process as it works for me. However, it still never fails that people will be set on who they want to come through and forget everyone else who has passed. One of the others who has passed can be a bridge to the one you were hoping to talk to so always validate if it fits anyone in your family.

For any medium to do his or her job well and for you to walk away with an awesome experience along with healing and peace, then please do the homework. It will be such a better experience.

8. What should you expect in a reading?

My intention is to provide an opportunity for your loved ones to come through with details about who is coming through, which for me includes: How they are related to you; their personality traits; how they passed; how your relationship was with them; and things that have occurred since their passing.

You want to know, are they still with you? Are they still in pain? Do they forgive you? and other situations where you feel you need closure. No matter how good and highly recommended a medium is, we can only do our best work when clients come to the appointment prepared—fully ready for a session—then 99.9% of them will leave with a remarkable experience, which can be extremely healing and life changing.

9. Should you record the session?

I have learned that allowing recordings or providing recordings of sessions, even in large groups, can be very helpful. Because much information comes through, it's difficult to remember all that is being shared. If you try to take notes, this becomes a little over-whelming. I prefer my clients to be taken care of and allow them to just hear what comes through. Also, listening to the recording later allows for things that maybe couldn't be understood during the session but may make sense re-hearing it. It's been a blessing to get emails validating things that came through in a session. Some-times even years down the road.

There have been times when someone has shared the recording with another friend or family member and the parts that weren't clear had made sense because he or she knew the story, whereas my client did not. When a loved one came through and my client couldn't identify the person right then, but after hearing the session again was able to recall the loved one not originally recognized. I get names often, but can also be provided with details of the person, such as personality, cause of death, and stories that connected them, which is why it's important to write down those that have passed—even if you think they won't show up.

10. Are there things to do after the session?

My advice for you if it has been a significant loss and it's the first time to a medium, is to take care of yourself. Take the day off if you can and allow yourself to process the session. It can be very exhilarating as well as very emotional. You will not know how you will respond and it's important to allow it to unfold the way you need it to be.

Stay hydrated, take a walk, hot bath, or do something sooth-ing. This can be very beneficial because emotions that have been pushed beneath the surface may reveal themselves, and you may not have been expecting the old wounds to show up uninvited. If you have a therapist, a good friend, or family member that you can trust, ask that person to provide support for you. Listen to your body and go through your own process.

Many of my clients have shared that it takes about two weeks to process the messages and for everything to sink in. Everyone has his or her time frame. It's important that you allow your time frame to be what you need it to be.

11. What does it cost?

In regard to cost, what should you expect to pay? Why are some mediums so expensive and others are not? I have had people ask me why I charge if this is a "gift" and even tell me that I "should" help people without charging. Well, that would be wonderful if I could do it for free and I'm sure most healers would love not to charge their clients, but like everyone, we have expenses to pay. I'm not sure if my bank would like for me to say, "hey, I'm a healer. Can I have my house for free?" I think they would laugh at me. As I shared earlier, it's an ability, and we all have abilities we share in exchange for payment. If you are a CPA, musician, doctor or hair stylist, money is the exchange of energy we as humans have created.

Only you can decide what medium and price you are willing to spend on the experience. As in any business, the more clients and the more recognition you have, the cost can change. Individuals have a choice as to whom they seek out, what their expectations are, how long they are willing to wait, as well as what they are willing to pay. Always trust your intuition, it's the best thing you have. For many of my clients and I'm sure other mediums have had similar responses, they will share that the session was like having two years of therapy. I'm always honored that the process can help with their healing, but always know that it's only one portion of the tools to help manage the loss of a loved one.

Suicide Statistics … Silent No Longer

Below are recent suicide statistics. These statistics have remained silent to most of us but they need to be front and center. As a society, we all need to be aware of these staggering numbers. And we need to support those afflicted with this terrible mental illness. How else can we begin to change the outcomes? What can you personally do to make these numbers decline?

Did you know…?

- Suicide is the 10th leading cause of death in the US

- Each year 44,965 die by suicide

- For every suicide, an estimated 25 attempt it

- Suicides cost the U.S. $69 billion annually

- On average, there are 105 to 123 suicides per day.

- Firearms account for 51% of all suicides.

- White males accounted for 7 of 10 suicides in 2016.

- The rate of suicide is highest in middle-age white men.

- 494,169 people visited a hospital for injuries due to self-harm in 2016.

- Females attempt suicide twice as often as males.

- Males are 4 times more likely than females to die by suicide.

- The ratio of suicide attempts to suicide death in youth is estimated to be about 25:1 compared to 4:1 in the elderly.

- Depression affects 20-25% of Americans ages 18+ in a given year.

- The highest suicide rates in the U.S. are among whites, American Indians and Alaska Natives.

- Only half of all Americans experiencing an episode of major depression receive treatment.

- An estimated quarter million people become suicide survivors

- 1 in 100,000 children aged 10-14 die by suicide each year.

- 7 in 100,000 youths aged 15-19 die by suicide.

- 12.7 in 100,000 young adults aged 20-24 die by suicide.

- Suicide is the 3rd leading cause of death for Americans aged 15-24.

- Suicide is the 2nd leading cause of death in the world for those aged 15-24.

- Lesbian, gay, and bisexual kids are 3 times more likely than straight kids to attempt suicide at some point in their lives.

- 41% of trans adults said they had attempted suicide. 61% of trans people who were victims of physical assault had attempted suicide.

- Lesbian, gay, and bisexual young people who come from families that reject or do not accept them are over 8 times more likely to attempt suicide than those whose families accept them.

- African American, Latino, Native American, and Asian American people who are lesbian, gay, or bisexual attempt suicide at especially high rates.

Resources

Sometimes you may not know where to start or what to ask for, however, I have listed a few sources that may get you started for yourself or the one you care about.

There are so many services available. Ask your doctor, psychologist, minister, friends, or simply Google. These organizations are experts in assisting and helping those you love to heal from your loss.

Many time hospitals will have free support groups. Surprisingly, mortuaries provide these helpful services, too.

And there is always Google. You have so much information at your fingertips now. Please research more resources in your area.

American Foundation for Suicide Prevention (AFSP)
Locate chapters in all 50 states. If in crisis, call National Suicide Prevention Lifeline
PHONE: 800-273-8255 (TALK)
TEXT: TALK to 7417410
WEBSITE: https://AFSP.org/

Bereaved Parents of the USA National Office
PHONE: 845-462-2825
WEBSITE: https://www.BereavedParentsUSA.org
ADDRESS: Katherine Corrigan
5 Vanek Road, Poughkeepsie, NY 12603-5403

Family: England, Wales and Scotland
PHONE: 800-029-2081-0800

Living Works

PHONE: 888-733-5484

EMAIL: info@LivingWorks.net

WEBSITE: www.LivingWorks.net

National Alliance on Mental Illness (NAMI)

PHONE: 800-950-6264

TEXT: NAMI to 741741

WEBSITE: https://www.NAMI.org

Psych Central: U.S. Helplines

PHONE - SUICIDE: 800-784-2433

PHONE - DEPRESSION SUPPORT GROUP: 800-826-3632

PHONE - SUICIDE PREVENTION SERVICES CRISIS HOTLINE:
800-784-2433

Prevention of Young Suicide UK | PAPYRUS

WEBSITE: https://www. PAPYRUS-uk.org

Suicide Prevention Lifeline

PHONE: 800-273-8255

WEBSITE: www.SuicidePreventionLifeline.org

The Compassionate Friends

PHONE: 630-990-0010

TOLL-FREE: 877-969-0010

WEBSITE: https://www.CompassionateFriends.org

WEBSITE: https://www.TCF.org.uk

Going it, and doing it, alone isn't the answer. There is no shame is asking for help during a time of grief, depression, or suicidal thoughts.

Acknowledgments

To my children Sophia and Jake who were supportive of the words that are shared and for the courage to experience so much in their young lives and have become two of the kindest souls I know.

Rashke Catlin who gave me an opportunity to be on her show at *KOSI 101.1* without having a practice. She opened a big door during an important crossroad for our family.

Judith Briles, The Book Shepherd, Editor and Commander in Chief, who took on this project that was a raw transcript and helped make it what it is today. Her openness and support made this possible.

Chris Sheppard who walked this path with us as we navigated through loss, healing and promise.

My brother, Darold and his lovely wife Lisa who have supported me every step of my entire life with only unconditional love.

My parents Bob and Fern who helped my children during their most difficult life experience. For my mother who gave me her sense of humor and my father who taught me to have good ethics.

My Aunt Bobbie and Uncle Buster who have always been very supportive of me and have loved me unconditionally. They are actually my cousins but I always called them aunt and uncle. I grew up with their three children and throughout our lives, we have had a very close relationship. Their son Robert was like a brother to me and passed 20 years ago. We all miss him very much.

My father-in-law Major General Jack Sheppard who was without a doubt my biggest cheerleader in my work and as his daughter in law. As I write this today, I'm sad to share he passed while this book was being completed in his home, April 2018.

Because of what I believe I know he is with all those we love including our beloved dogs. Jack supported also by sending an endless supply of pens, calendars and advertising material to support my business. He will be deeply missed.

To my clients, guides, loved ones who are in spirit that have continued to support me to be a messenger in both worlds.

To all my special friends that have watched my journey and have been in my life at the perfect time. There are many that have touched my heart and I'm forever grateful to them.

To both Brad and Mat that led me to understanding and allowed me to share about loss, grief, healing and of course mental illness.

Dana Nieto, that I believe was sent to me from this incredible universe to help me with our children, Sophia, Jake and Thomas and our four fur babies. I truly believe that this book would not be in your hands if it wasn't for her deep heart and unconditional love for me and those we hold close to us. I also believe she has saved my life many times.